# THE GIFT OF KINDNESS

Pam Ahern is the founder and director of Edgar's Mission, a not-for-profit sanctuary that provides a safe haven for over 300 rescued animals. She gave up her day job and a successful equestrian career to dedicate her life to the protection of farmed animals.

Edgar's Mission was established on 60 peaceable acres near Kilmore, Victoria. In ten years, thousands of farmed animals have been given a second chance at life after having made their way through the farm gates.

"Our greatest
glory is not in
never falling, but in
rising
every time
we fall"

Confucius (551-479 BC)

# THE GIFT OF KINDNESS

## Pam Ahern

Photography by Kyle Behrend

PENGUIN BOOKS

*To Edgar Alan Pig, a humble
being, a wise muse and a
dear friend. You taught me
the gift of kindness and,
because of you, I strive to
be a better version of myself
each and every day.*

# Contents

# Welcome to Edgar's Mission

If you had asked me a little over ten years ago where I would be today, I strongly doubt I would have said, 'Rescuing and caring for farm animals and spreading a message of kindness.' There is a wonderful quote that states, 'I may not have gone where I intended to go, but I think I have ended up where I needed to be.' And when I reflect back over all my life has been, I think this statement sums it up perfectly.

When I was younger, all I wanted to do was ride horses and have a pony of my very own. I guess that is pretty much every animal-loving girl's dream. But my folk were city folk and ours wasn't a particularly well-off family, so my pleadings for a pony fell on deaf ears. But to quote my mother, 'The worst thing you can say to Pam is "You can't".' I wasn't a particularly belligerent child, but I relished a challenge then, just as I relish a challenge now. It's all about that indefinable moment when you dare to ask, 'What if?'

I was never allowed a pushbike because my mother considered it to be far too dangerous. So, being an intrepid five-year-old, I removed my scooter's tyres. I 'borrowed' a pair of my mum's pantyhose, and tied a tyre to each end. I then fashioned this ingenious contraption into a saddle straddling the kitchen stool. Years later, I guess my mum got sick of never having any pantyhose so she took me off to the local pony club. And it was there that the foundations were laid for my association with farm animals.

In 2003 I had another, 'What if?' moment when I met someone who changed my life forever. That someone was a gentle pig I came to love and adore; I named him Edgar Alan Pig. It was during one of those tender moments we spent together in his stable, me rubbing his tummy and him offering his enthusiastic piggy grunts, that I had my most profound 'What if?' moment.

I am sure all of you have had a special animal in your life who touched your heart like no other. For all intents and purposes, Edgar was just like everyone's beloved pet except for one stark reality — he looked different to the usual dog, cat, bird and so on. As I got to know my Edgar, I quickly realised that the differences were limited only to outward appearances. And I learned that these differences most certainly did not justify the way our society treats the animals we farm for food and fibre.

And so, challenging all those who insisted, 'You can't,' I gave up my fulltime paying job. I hung up the riding boots on my successful equestrian career. I bade farewell to my partner of ten years when he posed the ultimatum, 'It's me or the pig.' I said goodbye to ever having a 'normal life' as I threw caution to the wind and decided to dedicate my life to the protection of farmed animals, because I did not want to reach the age of 85 and think, 'What if?'

Ten years on, thousands of farmed animals have been given a second chance at life after making their way through our farm gates. Not only have we given these creatures a life worth living, we have also given many of them their very first taste of human kindness. But I like to think Edgar's Mission has been able to achieve much more than just this, in that it has also been able to change the way people view farmed animals. Through our outreach work, humane education programs and farm tours, thousands upon thousands of people have had the chance to get up close and personal with farmed animals and in doing so, have had cause to question many of their long-held beliefs and practices.

At any given moment, farmed animals sit on the sidelines of our lives as well as our ethical and moral decisions. These are animals whose lives we determine with those very same decisions, yet we never see their suffering. There can be no doubt that recognising the animals we farm for food and fibre as individual, emotional creatures with the potential to lead happy, meaningful lives causes many people to realise that our current animal protection laws, along with the exemptions they contain, cannot possibly be justified.

I take great comfort in knowing that by giving a voice to my farm animal friends, we are able to speak to hearts and change minds. After all, if we could live happy and healthy lives without harming others, why wouldn't we?

# Edgar Alan Pig
## The Pig Who Started It All

When James Cromwell, Farmer Hoggett from the hit movie *Babe*, arrived in Australia in May 2003, it seemed like a golden opportunity to highlight the plight of pigs and put the spotlight on our flawed animal protection legislation that says some animals are more equal than others. James, a passionate animal activist, readily agreed to help. We thought it would be a good idea to get a photograph of James and a pig. But where would we find a pig?

An approach to a children's farm revealed that if we parted with $150 they would be happy to let James have his photo taken with a pig. 'Pigs!' we said, and then had the brilliant idea of procuring our own pig. And procure we did, from a piggery, a landrace large white cross who we named Edgar Alan Pig. A sanctuary was then needed to provide lifelong loving care for our porcine star. So we created such a sanctuary and named it Edgar's Mission in his honour, and life for all changed forever. Today literally thousands of animals' lives have been saved thanks to this humble pig.

Pam took Edgar for walks in the park and people would come from everywhere to marvel at his unique brand of pigginess. With his deep guttural belly grunts, Edgar quickly endeared himself to all he met. Watching the profound effect Edgar had on people — way beyond anything she could say — Pam came to thinking that the best ambassadors for changing the way people think about farmed animals were the animals themselves. So Edgar's Mission became a sanctuary for the animals who could be rescued and a much-needed voice for those who could not. Edgar's delightful ability to champion the cause of pigs saw him become the first in a great line of ambassador pigs who now call Edgar's Mission home sweet home.

Sadly, Edgar passed on shortly after his seventh birthday party. He is still missed but his mission will continue.

'I like pigs. Dogs look up to us.
Cats look down on us. Pigs treat us as equals.'
— *Sir Winston Churchill*

# Ginger
## Good Things Come in Small Packages

Late one summer evening, following the sound of noisy chirps, inquisitive and caring human ears were drawn to a tiny ball of yellow fluff beneath some bushes in a suburban backyard. How a tiny chick made its way to this most unlikely of resting spots will never be known and a doorknock of neighbouring households shone no light on the mystery. What did shine brightly, however, was the kindness of the human heart in rescuing Ginger the chirping chicken.

So named after the heroine hen from *Chicken Run*, the movie, Ginger has done what all hens yearn to do: to cheat their grisly fate that is predetermined by humans. Just like her namesake in the movie, young Ginger's affable and forthright personality touches all she meets. While many chickens look the same, their personalities are as individual as humans, something that is obvious to all whose hearts have been touched by a feathered friend.

Ginger Chick made clear her likes and dislikes. Among her likes were grapes, warm places, trotting across keyboards, singing

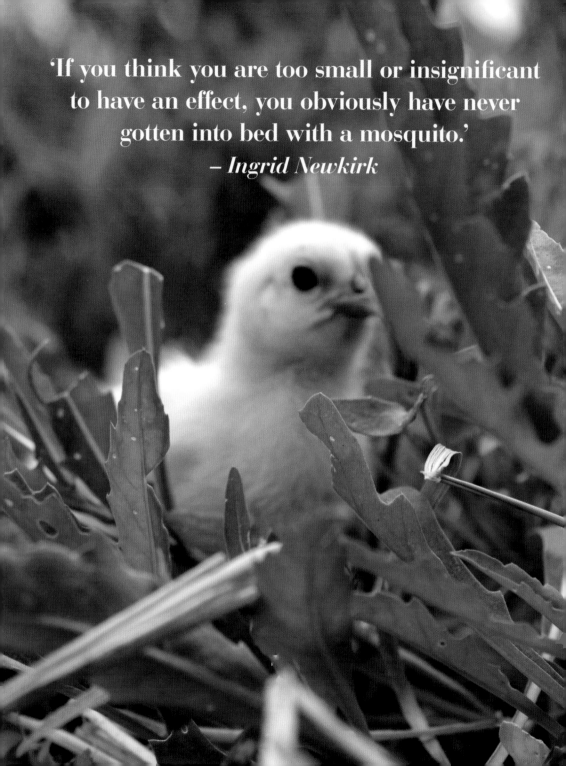

'If you think you are too small or insignificant to have an effect, you obviously have never gotten into bed with a mosquito.'
– *Ingrid Newkirk*

happy chicken songs, perching on shoulders and pecking at ears. Luckily for Ginger, her dislikes were few and short lived; like being placed into her pet carrier at bedtime which meant she couldn't cosy up to the humans she had come to know.

When we look at this petite and vulnerable creature, it is hard to fathom how mankind could ever set out to wrong one so innocent. But sadly, humans do wrong by the Gingers of this world far too often, using farming methods that are unfathomable to a kind heart.

A male chick born into the egg industry is deemed to be of no economic value and is discarded at only one or two days old. Conservative estimates show that well over 12 million baby chicks, just like Ginger, are killed every year in Australia by this industry simply because they are born male. The truth is, that for every egg-laying hen within this industry, there is a tiny male version of Ginger who did not make it.

And while many may argue what came first, the chicken or the egg, one thing is for sure: the fate of sweet chicks like Ginger rests with the goodness of the human heart.

# Alan Marshall
## He Can Jump Puddles

The last thing we wanted to do late on a Friday night after an exhausting week was to hit the road again. But a tiny lamb was in need. He had been found by the side of the road, no sheep or farm in sight. The tiny bundle of life was quickly ferried to an outer Melbourne veterinary clinic where the call was made to Edgar's Mission.

Our hearts sank when we saw the pitiful fellow. Unable to stand on horrifically crippled legs and unable to see through pus-encrusted eyes, his chance of survival looked slim. But he was determined to live, so we were determined to assist. If lambs are not well nourished they will quickly dehydrate and in severe cases this will cause the eyes to sink. That's what had happened to dear Alan, resulting in a condition called entropion where the eyelids turn in upon themselves causing the lashes to scratch the surface of the lens. Despite being only hours old, ulcers and infection had already taken hold.

The first of Alan's ailments were addressed: eyes bathed with a mild saline solution, cream administered and massaging commenced.

With regular physiotherapy, young Alan grew stronger every day — his love of life was obvious to anyone who met this precocious and effervescent lamb. Alan is a reminder that no matter how fearful the odds may seem, there is always a reason for hope and the need to jump puddles.

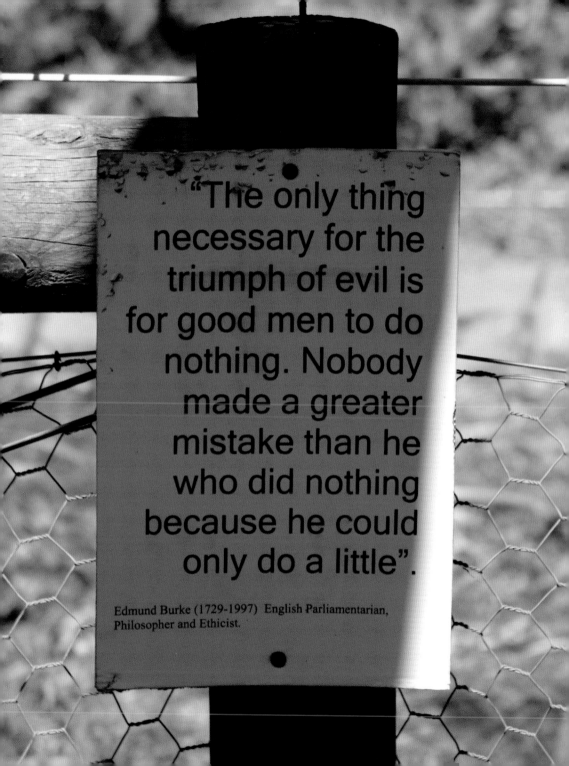

"The only thing necessary for the triumph of evil is for good men to do nothing. Nobody made a greater mistake than he who did nothing because he could only do a little".

Edmund Burke (1729-1997) English Parliamentarian, Philosopher and Ethicist.

# Monty
## The Big Little Pony

*Q: When does being small mean not being small enough? And your penalty is your death?*

*A: When you have been bred to be a miniature pony and it soon becomes apparent that you will not be quite miniature enough.*

That was the lot of dear little Monty Pony. When he was just five months old, Monty's breeders realised that he would grow too tall to meet the height requirements of the miniature pony breed. Rather than take responsibility for the life they created, the breeders were planning to send Monty to the knackery. This is the fate endured by many animals who do not live up to the expectations of their breeders.

Luckily for dear little Monty a kind hearted lady bravely intervened. At great personal expense she persuaded (and it took much persuasion) the breeders to spare Monty's life and allow her to rescue him. He now spends his days at Edgar's Mission as the official tour guide and complementary handbag searcher.

# 8 Lucky Turkeys
## A Christmas Tale

There was movement in the barn for word had passed around that Christmas time was coming and people's compassion had got away . . .

When eight turkeys escaped their fate and were in need of lifelong sanctuary, Edgar's Mission was only too pleased to open their barn doors to the chirping brood. At just a few weeks old Paul Keating, John Howard, Winston Churchill, Gordon Brown, David Cameron, John Major, James Callaghan and Margaret Thatcher all took to their new digs like ducks to water . . . or rather like turkeys to, um, Christmas.

While many people associate Christmas and turkeys, if this plucky octet have their way, people's hearts and minds will be opened to an entirely new meaning for peace and goodwill, without a gentle bird being the centrepiece of the dinner table!

Turkeys are noble, inquisitive and friendly creatures, considered by Benjamin Franklin far more worthy to be the national bird of America than the bald eagle. You would know this if you have ever

'All of us have the power to give happiness … a listening ear, a seeing eye, an outstretched hand.'

– *Pam Brown*

# The Lowdown on Turkeys

Turkeys are curious and intelligent animals. They suffer physical pain, just as humans and other animals do. They also experience similar emotional states to humans, including fear, anxiety, frustration, boredom, pleasure and enjoyment.

In developed countries, more than 90 per cent of commercial turkey production takes place in confined animal feeding operations, otherwise known as factory farms. Sadly, in Australia an average of three to five million turkeys are killed annually for meat, with Australians each eating around one kilo of turkey meat per year. And yes, most of this takes place at Christmas.

Turkeys born into the meat industry will bear little resemblance to their wild cousins; hatched from an incubator instead of a loving mother, they will be unable to fly and due to the unnatural heavy muscle mass of their chests they are unable to mate naturally. When they are one day old, they are packed into a 'grower' shed with 10–14,000 of their kind. On average, there are six birds per square metre of space – imagine each bird living its life on an A3-sized sheet of paper.

In confinement, turkeys are unable to do what their instincts tell them to: spread their wings, fly, perch, forage, run, and simply breathe fresh air and feel the sun. Confined in sheds with artificial lighting that distorts normal sleeping and feeding patterns, and sitting upon a continual build-up of excrement, these turkeys are prone to serious health and welfare issues such as lameness, skin diseases and eye disorders. Their living conditions cause them to become increasingly bored and frustrated, leading to fighting between individuals who would otherwise be friends. To 'solve' this fighting, young babies have the ends of their beaks and the ends of their toes cut off, a painful procedure performed without any anaesthetic or pain relief.

The young birds are often fed antibiotics to control diseases that could spread rapidly in such cramped conditions, and to fatten them up.

The saddest thing of all is that factory farmed turkeys never live a long and happy life. Females are generally killed at around 10 weeks of age, weighing approximately 5 kilos, while males are slaughtered at around 17 weeks young. Turkeys should live for up to ten years.

# Lucky Bunny
## Getting a Second Chance

With Christmas fast approaching and New Year just around the corner, animal shelters were quickly filling and had little room for yet another unwanted white bunny. Luck was fast hopping away when Lucky Bunny's numbers came up — she happened to be sitting forlornly at a vet clinic when Edgar's Mission staffers called to collect a wayward duck.

Lucky Bunny was friendly, curious and most deserving of a second chance at life and we determined to give her just that. Bunnies like Lucky endure so much hardship in our world; they can be factory farmed for food and fibre, have cruel experiments performed on them and people often get them as novelty pets. The novelty usually wears off long before the rabbit's life does.

We can all make the world a kinder place for bunnies by refusing to wear fur, never eating rabbit meat (factory farmed or otherwise), ditching cosmetics and household products that have been tested on animals and not taking a bunny into your world unless you are prepared to give him or her the life they deserve.

# Othello
## Where the Grass is Greener

Othello is a modern-day tragedy, albeit with a happy ending. Othello and his two buddies somehow found their way onto a busy outer Melbourne freeway. Terrified and way out of their depth, the trio didn't know which way to run. Sadly Othello's two offsiders took a chance to flee across the busy thoroughfare and fell victim to a motor vehicle. Left alone and scared, Othello somehow became entangled in a discarded tarpaulin and things went from bad to worse in the blink of eye. But luckily the goodness of the human heart came to the fore.

Othello's plight reached local wildlife carers who enlisted the help of Manfred and his dart gun. The heavily sedated goat then gave his rescuers more than a few anxious moments as he struggled to come out of the sedation. Arriving at Edgar's Mission still unconscious, it was to be a long night monitoring Othello's vital signs. He reaped the benefits of many previous hours, days and months spent rehabilitating goats who had justifiably lost their trust of man. Through the dawn rays, Othello staggered about the stable like a drunken sailor, trying to flee despite his disabled state. He was convinced ours was a species not to be trusted. But the Lady with the Hat was patient and kind with a gentle touch. She spent many hours just sitting with Othello until the day came for him to once again reacquaint himself with the outside world.

With great trepidation Othello followed his new buddy, and mixing trust with skittishness, headed for a laneway brimming with luscious long grass. The goat and his friend explored, Othello agreeing, 'The grass here really is greener.' When the Lady with the Hat departed, it wasn't long before Othello jumped the fence and tagged along. When office jobs beckoned, another yard was found with an even higher fence. Othello enjoyed his new digs until once again, the Lady with the Hat departed and he proved that a higher fence was no impediment for his love. It took a cyclone fence, a small enclosure and a steely resolve to find a yard that could contain Othello long enough for him to recover before he could be introduced to his new goaty buddies. He has learned to make do with joyous short interludes of tagging along, assisting the Lady with the Hat on her rounds of the farm.

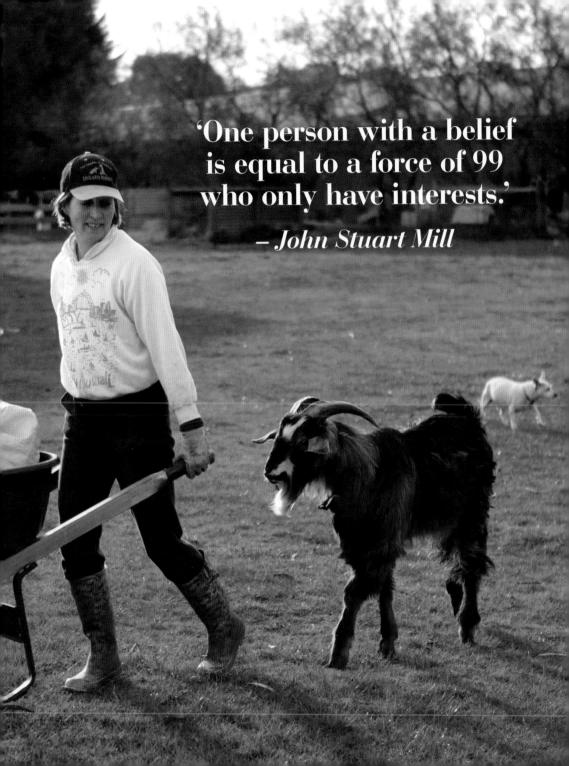

'One person with a belief
is equal to a force of 99
who only have interests.'

– *John Stuart Mill*

# Coco

## How Much is That Ducky in the Window?

Millions of hapless hounds know the real cost of that doggie in the pet shop window: cute puppy morphs into boisterous shoe-chewing canine and the novelty is gone. With our community already struggling to cope with the burgeoning number of unwanted cats and dogs, it seems bizarre that we are adding more and more species to the mix of abandoned pets. Adorable Coco was purchased on a whim by a schoolgirl who soon realised she couldn't care for her, so the tiny bundle was passed around school friends. Realising that 'pass the duckling' was no life for a sweet little creature, the call was made to Edgar's Mission.

Mother Nature knows best and a mother duck would teach her brood important life lessons for up to 12 weeks before the ducklings became fully independent. So the task fell to her human carers at Edgar's Mission. Until Coco's water repellent feathers emerged she would be vulnerable to the elements. With no protective mother duck's wing to retreat under, Coco needed to be protected from the elements and to never feel lonely.

# Burpy
## Wilbur the Celebrity Pig

On 26 November 2006 as a tiny six-week-old piglet, Burpy, aka Wilbur, walked the red carpet at the Royal Theatre in Melbourne with Hollywood star Dakota Fanning as special guests at the world premier of the movie *Charlotte's Web*. A photo of Wilbur being cuddled by Dakota was in the *Herald Sun*; he was mobbed at the after party by adoring fans, and he even graced the news services that night.

Now such instant fame might have gone to many a pig's head, but not Burpy. He realised how lucky he was to have been plucked from obscurity to become a star. You see, Burpy was no different to any other pig, except that he was getting to lead the life that all pigs deserve. Burpy could have wallowed in his new-found fame at Edgar's Mission and not done another day's work, but he chose differently. Realising he had a personal mission to embark upon, he chose to meet as many people as possible and remind them of the important message contained in the story of *Charlotte's Web*.

*Charlotte's Web* is a classic story of loyalty, trust and sacrifice. The little girl, Fern, is one of only two living beings who sees that Wilbur, the runt of the litter, is a special animal as she raises him into a terrific and radiant pig. As Wilbur moves into a new barn, he begins a second profound friendship with the most unlikely of creatures — a spider named Charlotte — and their bond inspires the animals around them to come together as a family.

When the word gets out that Wilbur's days are numbered, it seems that only a miracle will save his life. A determined Charlotte — who sees miracles in the ordinary — spins words into her web in an effort to convince the farmer that Wilbur is 'some pig' and worth saving.

The most important and powerful line in the movie is 'I want to live!' Wilbur had just found out that he was going to be killed for Christmas dinner. That didn't make sense to him. He had so much to do, so much to experience, and he had friends he wanted to grow old with! And he couldn't understand why anyone would want to hurt him. But Wilbur was a lucky pig because his friends joined forces to save his life and in doing so made a whole town realise what remarkable living beings pigs are, rather than only thinking of what remains when their life is ended: pork, ham and bacon.

But the most important message that Wilbur tries to get people to understand is that animals feel joy and sorrow, pain and fear, in the same way that we do, and they respond to kindness — in the same way that we do.

Today, a rather larger version of that tiny piglet who captured the hearts of people all around the world lounges about the farm living the life of Riley and making choices, his choices. What a lucky pig!

"All things are possible until they are proved impossible — and even then the impossible may only be so as of now"

*Pearl S. Buck*

Oh, and why Burpy? Well, because when Burpy arrived at Edgar's Mission, there was already a pig named Wilbur and because pigs are so smart and quickly learn their names, we didn't want to confuse them. So we shortened Wilbur to just Bur, but when the little fella ate too much he would burp . . .

This wonderful movie and the words of author E.B. White gave a voice to what so many farm animals would say if they could speak. 'I want to live.' 'I can't understand why you would want to hurt me.' 'Living is just as important to me as it is to you!'

# Bubbles & Babe
## Seeing the World Differently

In the Shakespearian tragedy *King Lear*, the blind Duke of Gloucester stood on the heath and when Lear's son-in-law asked how he saw the world he replied, 'I see the world feelingly.'

On 19 August 2009 two tiny, five-week premature white lambs arrived at Edgar's Mission, blind from birth. Although most of us would consider this a major disability, Bubbles and Babe saw themselves as nothing other than two normal little lambs who just wanted to get on with life.

Bubbles was so-named for all the frothy bubbles she created while feeding and Babe, the stronger of the two, was just one sweet little babe. With a birth weight of just a couple of kilos between them it was a miracle they made it. The lively pair spent their evenings in a pet carrier by the fire and their daytime was spent in either a square enclosure or hanging out with the bunnies, if the weather was inclement.

Each day saw them growing stronger and gaining weight. We madly chased them about the kitchen each morning to put their little

There is only one thing worse than being blind and that is being able to see and yet have no vision

Helen Keller

jackets on. They were two of the cuddliest lambs we have ever come across and quickly instructed us that they must be cuddled for at least ten minutes after feeding. To watch them both, heads held high and outstretched, eyes closed, engulfed in blissful oblivion was a true slice of heaven.

Would they ever be able to see? The simple answer is we didn't know. We thought it may have been some neurological condition caused by their premature birth. That their mother rejected them at birth was indicative of Mother Nature's knowledge that these little two darlings would never have been able to cope in a 'normal' sheep's world.

We looked out the window to catch a glimpse of two dear little blind baby lambs gambolling in a rare moment of sunshine, seeing the world feelingly.

# Claudette
## Patience is a Virtue

Claudette had been on the run for over eight weeks before being captured in an outer eastern Melbourne suburb. She was terrified of humans as some people had been very cruel to her and she didn't trust anyone. Somehow, while she was on the run one of her horns had broken off very close to her skull. It bled and bled, and she had dried blood all over her face and the exposed horn bud was very sore. The pain made her even more scared of everything.

Once she was captured she did her best to flee but she couldn't escape. She was taken to an animal hospital where they treated her horn and fed and watered her but she couldn't stay there. They were unsure about where to send her because she was just so scared of everything, and someone even suggested she should be put to sleep. Perhaps they knew she had trouble sleeping at nights because she would remember all the awful things that had happened to her. When people came to check on her during the day she would tremble with fear, sometimes standing on her back legs and charging at the humans before they had a chance to do anything awful to her.

Then someone called Edgar's Mission. They said they would take her, knowing that her physical injuries would soon heal very well and that the real test of her recovery would be the psychological damage.

At first she would tremble uncontrollably whenever anyone came near her. She would try to jump out of the stable to flee. But the Lady in the Hat was kind and patient, often just sitting in the stall and letting the terrified goat sniff her. Slowly Claudette grew to trust the lady and they became buddies, even going for walks together. It took longer with the other people.

Some of us are slower to get to know than others, for a whole lot of reasons. Be patient, it's often worth the wait.

'Nothing is more powerful than an idea whose time has come.'

— *Victor Hugo*

# Hansel
## A One-in-a-Million Baby

It is a fresh, cool spring morning and as the sun rises on a brand new day, a loving mother gently tends to her newborn. She caresses him, protects him from harm and guides him to nurse from her. Already bonded from his time within the womb, the baby trusts her tender guidance, and so he begins to suckle. His instinct tells him to draw in the essential life-giving sustenance that only his mother's milk can provide.

But no sooner does the warm sweet taste of nourishment fill his mouth than he is torn away. Strong arms wrap their way around his body and hoist him far away from the soft gentle teat that calls to him. His mother, try as she may, cannot dislodge her precious baby from the thief's arms and she earns a rough sharp hand on her side for her efforts. She cries out for her baby, feeling pain that only a mother can. She will cry for days and the pain of her loss will last for much longer. She will not forget the one who stole her baby away. And her baby cries for her, confused and scared, having lost the only security he had ever known.

What kind of animal would take a baby away from his mother? What kind of animal would take away the one source of nourishment that baby needed to begin his life? What kind of animal would break one of the strongest and most precious bonds to exist upon our earth? We would. We humans. We created the dairy industry and along with it, we created stories just like this one.

But somebody was watching over this one-in-a-million baby on that fateful day. Someone was filled with kindness and saw that this baby calf needed to be rescued. And so, after some negotiation, a last-minute reprieve was granted and the baby was loaded into a spacious van filled with soft straw, provided with essential nourishment and water and began his journey toward a future that was worth a whole lot more than a measly bob.

He was christened Hansel. He shared his new life at Edgar's Mission with another young calf named Gretel. Gretel had also survived against the odds, having been born with only three legs.

They lived their younger days being lovingly hand-raised and bottle-fed, and Hansel and Gretel now reside together, living a life of luxury that they would never have dreamt possible. Wide open spaces surround them and they will never see the inside of a dusty market pen, nor will they be handled by rough hands ever again. Instead, kind hands proffer much loved massages and trails of breadcrumbs lead them not to houses of gingerbread, but to lush green pastures where they happily graze their days away.

And so, it is on a fresh, cool spring morning and as the sun rises on a brand new day, Hansel, one-time bobby calf, awakens to feel strong arms wrapping around his body yet again. But he does not flinch, nor does he feel any fear or trepidation. For these strong arms simply offer a warm embrace, telling him he is loved. No longer a baby, this majestic creature steps out into the world, proof that the kindness of one can change a life. Proof that this life is worth a whole lot more than a single bob.

# The Lowdown on Cows

Cows are incredibly social animals. They form large herds and just like people, they will bond to some herd members while avoiding others.

Just like humans, cows use their voice and facial expressions to communicate how they are feeling. They are emotional and sensitive creatures that form close and long-lasting relationships.

Cows are curious and inquisitive. They babysit for one another and they can even hold grudges.

Recent research conducted at Cambridge University by Professor Donald Broom has shown that cows have 'Eureka' moments. Cows were challenged to open a door to get to food while their brainwaves were measured by an electroencephalograph. The results showed the cows clearly became excited when they discovered how to open the door.

Cows have exhibited further signs of intelligence by being taught to unlatch a gate for food, to follow signs to different areas and to push a certain lever when hungry and a different one when thirsty!

A dairy cow must have a calf in order to produce milk. After giving birth to a calf, she is soon impregnated again for the cycle to continue.

A dairy calf is separated from its mother soon after birth so that her milk may be harvested for human consumption. If given the chance, a calf would suckle from its mother for several months, even up to a year.

The mother–calf bond is particularly strong, and there are countless reports of mother cows who continue to frantically call and search for their babies after the calves have been taken away.

If a calf is born female, there is a chance she may be used as a herd replacement animal. However all male calves and many females are by-products of the dairy industry and are sent to slaughter soon after birth. These calves have been dubbed 'bobby calves'; they are seen as being worth only a 'bob' by the industry.

Almost one million calves taken from their mothers by the dairy industry were slaughtered in Australia in 2010.

Although a cow may live for up to 20 years, the lifespan of a dairy cow is only 7 years or even less as she is sent to slaughter when deemed no longer productive.

While a calf would normally suckle from its mother up to five times a day, Australian Standards and Guidelines allow a 5-day-old calf to be left for up to 30 hours without food during transport to and within slaughterhouses.

# The Two Ronnies
## Double the Fun

*The Two Ronnies* was a hit comedy series in the 1970s and 80s starring Ronnie Barker and Ronnie Corbett. They delighted millions with their unique sense of mirth and merriment. These two young vocal roosters were not such a hit, resulting in the two roosters being unceremoniously dumped at a children's farm. With no room for them at the inn, a call was made to Edgar's Mission.

The Two Ronnies stole the show as soon as they arrived at the farm. Almost inseparable, these spectacularly colored bantam Sussex roosters entertained visitors and volunteers with their cheeky antics. They appointed themselves as unofficial policemen of the sanctuary, busily and bossily chasing after any creature they felt was in the wrong place at the wrong time. Full of their own diminutive importance, this double act patrols the farm, chests puffed out and heads held high and heaven help any unsuspecting hen — they have even been known to lie in wait in a nesting box.

'Dance as though no-one is watching; love as though you've never been hurt; sing as though no-one is listening; live as though heaven is on Earth.'

# Rory
## The Best Friend

For as long as Rory can remember she has loved people. She loved the first lady in her life like no other, and didn't care that the lady found a human she wanted to spend her time with as it made her happy so Rory was happy too. Alas, the man didn't love Rory, and thought the lady spent too much time with her dog. He gave her an ultimatum: 'It's me or the dog.' Rory was scared. The lady took her the very next day to the vet, handed her lead to the nurse and walked out of her dog's life forever.

Rory was sad; she loved the lady. The nurse bent down and touched the dog's head, and a tear dropped from her cheek. Rory licked her hand and wished she wouldn't be sad. She sat down and pushed her back against the nurse's leg and looked up with her big brown eyes. 'No one should ever make anyone make such a choice,' the nurse told her colleague. 'It's not fair,' the other woman said, and her eyes too began to mist over. Rory was delivered to Edgar's Mission.

In animals, each human finds their measure; how we treat animals tells the world so much about the sorts of people we are. It's lucky for the boyfriend he wasn't taken to the vet, because there is no place at the mission for someone who would force another person to make such a decision.

'We are called to treat them with kindness, not because they have rights or power or some claim to equality, but because they don't.'

— *Matthew Scully*

# Bambi
## Out of the Woods

On Saturday 7 February 2009 a single event changed the lives of many Victorians. We now know it as Black Saturday and it will long haunt the memories of thousands of people. Out of the ashes of despair, acts of kindness flourished alongside incredible tales of survival.

Bambi was a tiny fawn who emerged from the blackened forest. Orphaned by the unforgiving fire, he was dazed, scared and suffering smoke inhalation and dehydration. The little fallow deer wandered the roadside. Placing their own loss and heartache aside, Kinglake residents rescued Bambi and took him to the RSPCA for emergency care.

Just a few weeks old, Bambi encapsulated the Australian spirit and refused to give up. Nine days on a drip and he was ready to face the challenge of learning to live without his mother's guiding touch. A sad fact of life for most deer is that there is no utopian forest for them to roam. A single word holds their fate — venison.

Bambi frolics in the sun at Edgar's Mission and shelters from the storms with never a threat of a hunter to take his sunshine away.

# Hope
## Prancing on Clouds

Christmas is never a good time for a pig, with all that ham and roast pork around. Hope was a very smart pig and so when the opportunity arose, she made her escape from the pig farm. It took a bit of work, lots of squeezing, hiding and running. Finally she reached the highway. She looked around and blinked in the sunshine, and although she had scratches and cuts she felt a million dollars. She took a deep breath and for the first time in her life her lungs filled with clean fresh air and it tasted so good. For the first time her delicate little trotters touched soft grass and it felt like she was prancing on clouds.

For a moment she almost forgot her pain, and then her heart began to ache for the buddies she had left behind. So she made them a solemn promise as she trotted to freedom: 'I will tell your story.'

Racing about the busy highway, no one seemed to care about an escapee piglet so she started to look for somewhere to rest. The first house she went to had a large dog who chased her. People came out to see what all the fuss was about. 'A pig!' they squealed. 'Catch it!' She wasn't sure if these people were good or bad folk and took off, just in case. She ran and ran with thoughts of ham running through her mind, until she was trapped. She bit the hand that grabbed her. 'Quick, get a cage!' she heard one person roar, and soon her freedom was gone.

She had almost given up hope until someone said, 'Call Edgar's Mission.' Hearing that name, she did a little happy pig dance. Soon she took her first look at heaven on earth as the Lady in the Hat whispered she loved her and told her she was safe.

Hope became an Ambassador Pig, in the true spirit of the great Edgar Alan Pig. She travelled far and wide, showing people what wonderful, happy and intelligent animals pigs are. She eventually retired, spending her days lazing in the sun, kicking back in her wallow or curled up in her straw bed and taking time out to say hello to her buddies.

# Calamity Jane
## Or, Houdini, the Runaway Goat

This diminutive, female kid goat caused mayhem for city commuters as she darted around cars, over nature strips and across parklands. She did a stint of road patrol on the busy Tullamarine Freeway and surrounding inner-city roads. For several weeks she had been spotted on the loose and numerous reports of her sightings filled the airwaves. But such notoriety gave her no comfort and as time wore on her energy waned.

But she didn't do this to make people cross; she was frightened and people were chasing her, yelling. Some said they even wanted to eat her! Wouldn't you have been scared too?

Her escapades made her famous around the world. American online newspaper *The Huffington Post* ran with a story: 'Houdini, Runaway Goat in Australia, Prompts Wild Chase with Officials'. Leading United Kingdom media outlet, Reuters, reported: 'Police go on wild goose chase to track down runaway goat', with the major Australian

'The best things in life aren't things.'
– *Art Buchwald*

dailies also running stories about her. Exhausted from constantly exploring new frontiers, she was finally wrestled to the ground by a TV cameraman who had come along hoping to film her capture, not carry it out.

People around the world cheered when she was saved, glad she had been spared the fate of most goats.

Now you might think such fame would go to her head, but no, she was more than happy to have found new digs at Edgar's Mission where the only shooting that goes on is with a camera and the only yelling is 'weeeetbix!' which she has developed quite a taste for.

Calamity Jane has gladly surrendered life on the run for yummy treats and welcome visitors.

# Charles Darwin
## A New-Found Theory

Charles Darwin walks with a severe neck twist that causes him to look partially skyward. His left leg skis across the grass with each awkward step and his back legs don't follow his front. He survived a debilitating farm accident and his resolve to beat the odds touched the hearts of his farming family. Recognising that Charles would need ongoing care and a suitable paddock, the call was made to Edgar's Mission.

One look into Charles' eyes tells you that he very much wants to be alive, despite his awkward movements. And sure, he looks different to the other sheep, yet nothing has diminished his reason for being. He loves playing with his buddies in the sunshine, comes running as fast as he can when he sees the feed bucket and relishes the touch of human kindness, especially when it comes in the form of a good old back scratch.

The name Charles Darwin is synonymous with the well-postulated theories of evolution and survival of the most fitting. After meeting our woolly Charles, many will walk away with a new-found theory: all animals want, need, deserve and respond to one thing. Kindness.

# Merlin
## The Magical Sheep

Merlin came to us one winter's day in the arms of a farmer's wife. He had been discovered desperately trying to keep up with his buddies as the flock was rounded up for a regular drenching. His bloodied leg with the bone exposed said he was in strife.

As soon as he arrived, we raced him to veterinary assistance where it was revealed that little Merlin appeared to be an orphan and had been struggling for some time, hence his potty stomach and vulnerability to attack. The attack had occurred some days ago and the little fellow's leg was not just broken, it was shattered and the exposed bones meant the likelihood of infection was high.

We named him Merlin, not so much because he looked like a little wizard with a pompom of wool on his head, but because it was going to take a miracle for him to survive. But survive he did. After enduring several trips back and forth to the vet, little Merlin grew in confidence and built up strength each day. A plaster cast for his leg was

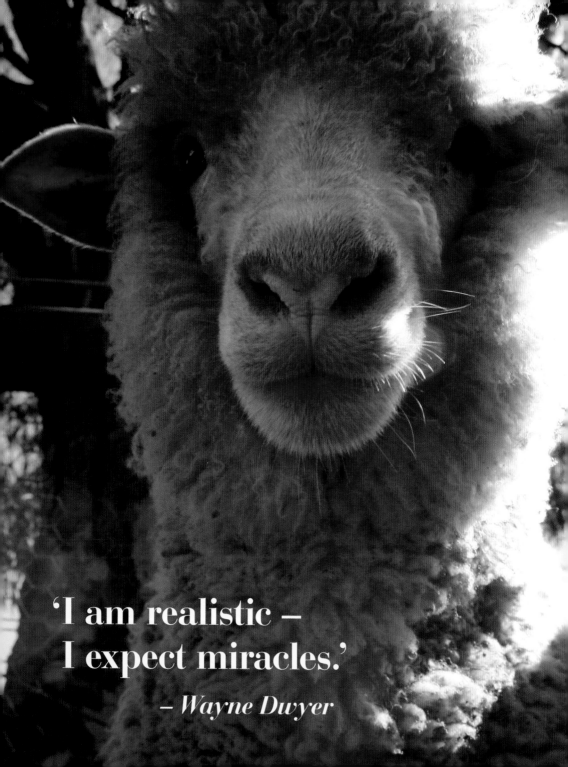

'I am realistic –
I expect miracles.'

– *Wayne Dwyer*

not possible initially due to the possibility of infection and the fact that the bones had shifted out of alignment. The cast would come later.

Despite Merlin being very young and requiring the life-sustaining milk of his mother, he had lost the sucking reflex of infants. Thankfully, all our past experience in raising orphans provided us with a wealth of knowledge that would help Merlin. At first syringing milk down his throat was difficult but history told us the little guy would come to not only accept this, but would look forward to it as a yummy treat. Merlin did not let us down.

Days rolled into weeks and soon Merlin was able to make the final journey to the vet to have his cast removed. With lots of physiotherapy and encouragement Merlin's little atrophied leg became useful once again. To look at Merlin today you would never think his life had hung in the balance.

# The Lowdown on Sheep

Sheep were among the first animals domesticated over 10,000 years ago with their primary ancestor being the wild Mouflon.

They have been selectively bred for economically important outcomes such as wool and meat. This has resulted in more than 1000 distinct breeds of sheep worldwide. The most common Australia breed is the Merino; at June 2011 this accounted for around 80 per cent of the nation's 73.1 million sheep herd.

Sheep are social animals who prefer to live together in groups called flocks. They have an excellent sense of hearing and are easily startled by loud noises.

The average lifespan of a sheep is 10 to 12 years, although they can live to be as old as 20 if given the chance. However most sheep and lambs are killed well before their time for economic purposes.

Sheep do not run feral in Australia because they do not have the ability to survive without human intervention. This evidence goes against claims that sheep are well adapted to the extremes of the Australian climate. Further proof of this comes from the fact that many sheep in Australia are subject to mulesing which sees pieces of flesh carved from the rear ends of young lambs in an attempt to prevent flystrike in this area. This highly controversial issue remains a huge welfare concern.

Australia sent just under 2.5 million sheep overseas as 'live' exports in 2011, with the Middle East taking over 99 per cent. This is despite many receiving countries having low or no enforceable animal welfare laws. The majority of the animals are slaughtered without stunning. Stunning is standard in all Australian abattoirs (with the exception of halal facilities).

The vast majority of animals exported live travel by sea on long haul journeys that can cause stress, injuries, illnesses and disease. Many animals die en route each year.

# Radar

## Miracle Boy

Radar was found along with his two siblings, Margaret and Hawkeye, by bushwalkers in Bacchus Marsh one cold June morning. They were all very weak, cold and hungry. No one knows exactly what happened to their mother. Hawkeye was the smallest and bravest of the three and wandered off to look for their mother but tumbled down a steep ravine. Luckily the bushwalkers heard his cries and came to save him and in doing so came across Radar and Margaret.

Abandoning their bushwalk, they bundled up the goats and promised to take them to a place of safety. They were still very cold, tired and hungry when the box lid opened and they took their first peek at Edgar's Mission. Sadly for Hawkeye and Margaret, salvation came too late and they passed away not long after our arrival. But they got to feel the touch of human kindness that Radar enjoys every day.

Like all mammals goats need their mother's milk in order to survive and most important is the colostrum (the first milk she produces). It is rich in energy, protein, vitamins and minerals, as it contains maternal antibodies that help protect newborns from disease. It is essential they receive it in their first 24 hours of life. Antibodies can only cross the intestinal wall and enter their bloodstream during the first 24 to 36 hours of life. For orphans like Radar, the susceptibility to diarrhoea and pneumonia is high if they don't get enough colostrum.

Radar's new human friends called him Miracle Boy because it was thought that the lost goats did not receive any colostrum and this may well be the reason for the rapid demise of Hawkeye and Margaret, despite the very best of care they received.

Radar may well be the miracle boy but the real miracle is the power of love and kindness.

"Don't be afraid that your life will end.
Be afraid that it will never begin."
– *Grace Hansen*

# Shirley
## The Ambassador for Bobby Calves

Shirley was taken from her mother not long after she was born. She was very small and the farmer didn't want her so she was sent to market. Things were not looking too good until she spotted a lady with a hat walking about the pens. The lady looked kind; she never shoved the calves like the other humans did, and didn't speak in a gruff voice. Shirley liked her from the start, and just watched until their eyes met.

Sadly there are around one million calves each year just like Shirley that find themselves at markets or worse. They are called bobby calves. The name bobby calf springs from the low value the dairy industry places on them, the forgotten ones. They are said to be 'only worth a bob', but we believe they are all priceless. Many people don't realise that mother cows, like all mammals, produce milk for their young and in order for mother cows to keep producing milk she needs to keep having a calf. The dairy industry might think bobby calves are 'a low value by-product of milk production' but it's not right for these small creatures to be considered nothing more than a production unit.

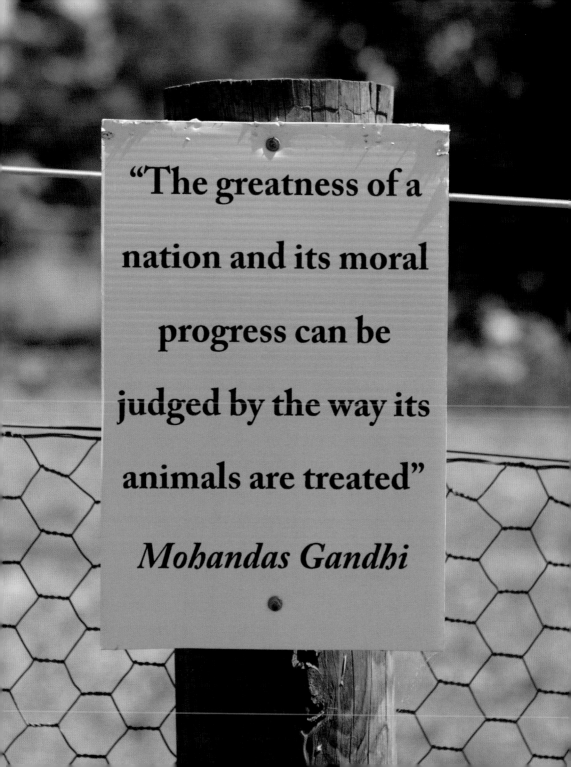

# Alice
## The Movie Star Pig

Alice arrived in the back of a trailer driven by her previous pig-farming owner. She had recently become a movie star, playing the mother of Wilbur in the Paramount Pictures production of E. B. White's classic *Charlotte's Web*. Alice was to be allowed to retire in 'wonderland'.

Alice stood in her trailer and took a tentative step onto solid earth: something completely unfamiliar to her, yet so natural for a pig. This one time factory-farmed sow had only ever known confinement, except for the hours she spent on the movie set. The pig farmer uttered, 'That's the first time she has eaten grass.' But Alice sure knew what to do with it, the same as she knew the earth was for rooting and the straw was for making a bed in. Rashes and sores on her side and rear end said they had never known the softness of anything other than concrete. Her sagging teats spoke of many litters and that her commercial use-by date was nigh. It was clear that human kindness was something foreign to her but she responded to it very quickly.

Alice was named in honour of Alice Walker, the black American writer and civil rights activist. Like her namesake, Alice Pig caused people to challenge and change popular thinking on what a pig's lot in life should be.

Alice lived out her life happily at Edgar's Mission unlike her brethren whose only taste of sunshine would come on the way to the slaughterhouse when they are so lame, ill or 'unproductive' that they are no longer capable of creating profit.

"The animals
of the world
exist for
their own
reasons. They
were not made
for humans any
more than
black people
were made for
white, or
women created
for men."
**Alice Walker**

# Chicquin
## Hatching a Good Idea

Many people are not aware that chickens can have personalities. That is, until they meet Chicquin, aka Super Chicken. Chicquin came into our lives after we received a call alerting us to the dire fate of a rooster who, should he not find a home within seven days, would be dealt with by order of the local council. It seemed that despite his endearing charm, his early morning vocal antics were not appreciated by neighbours. Having survived a school hatching project, Chicquin's lot was not looking good. Touched by the love and concern of his schoolgirl guardian, we readily agreed to offer Chicquin sanctuary at the mission, but little did we know what an incredibly personable bird he would be.

Kindly devising a new office filing system that only he could master was added to his list of administrative duties, which included crowing madly whenever the telephone rang and cheekily sitting on Pam's lap as she drove around the farm. Chicquin became famous in his ambassador role as he was incredibly attectionate and relished pats and cuddles. He was only too willing to show just how clever chickens can be, even recognising and answering to his name.

But Chicquin also told an important story of the sorry tale behind many a well-intentioned school hatching project. Despite good intentions, these projects neither teach lessons of compassion or responsibility to the impressionable young students, nor always ensure the chicks can live long and happy lives. Rather, they teach lessons of detachment, expendability and the view that animals are mere teaching aids. Life is trivialised as teacher and student do not always accept the grave and permanent responsibility of bringing a life into the world. And this is a world that already struggles to cope with an ever-growing number of unwanted cats and dogs, let alone adding roosters to the mix. A mother chicken will lovingly turn her egg many times during the day and night, will chirp to it and keep it safe and warm. This cannot be replicated in a school environment where excited children and lack of a veterinary budget see chicken welfare compromised.

Life with Chicquin was indeed a joyful pleasure and confirmed the wonderful nature of his much maligned species. It's easy to spend several hours entranced, watching the behaviour of these creatures as they busily go about the business of being a chicken and never appear bored.

There is so much to learn from animals. They teach us how to overcome limits imposed by difference, to live outside of words, to expand our awareness and to take responsibility for another living creature.

# Macho
## Man About the Farm

Macho is a term used to describe a male alpaca used for breeding. It is also the name of Edgar's Mission's first alpaca. The shy little jet black fellow with his funny lower bucked teeth was about 5 months old when he arrived at the farm. Far removed from his ancestors' homeland of South America, Macho, like his forefathers, settled in to his new home rather well. Quickly bonding with his sheepy friends, he followed them about the farm.

Alpacas belong to the camel family Camelidae, of the order Artiodactyla, which includes llamas, hippopotamuses, pigs, deer, giraffes, sheep, goats and cattle. Smaller than llamas, alpacas have a fleece that is much prized because of its economic benefits. Sadly for Macho and his buddies his previous owner only viewed these intelligent creatures for what they could produce rather than the unique animals they are. This was the case for emus about 20 years ago; they were a means to get rich quick, with owners tiring quickly when returns waned.

Macho and his mum had an owner with many things to worry about; tending his charges was clearly not one of them. They were housed in overcrowded paddock with too little feed and several of the herd died a slow, agonising death by starvation. Macho and his mum were quickly going this way too, until their rescue. Alpacas are noted for their ability to withstand harsh conditions over a long time, so one can only imagine the conditions of Macho's flock were pretty dire.

A testament to a mother's love, Macho's mum put everything into her son, but despite the best of care she died. Macho's legacy is stunted growth; he is very small for his age. With tender loving care, things have gone well for young Macho although he will never live up to his name by being a stud animal, because he has been castrated.

It didn't take Macho long to realise that we are the good guys. He meanders up for a closer inspection, but he also reminds us that it is on his terms, not ours, and if we venture too close he takes off. You can't help but smile as Macho looks deep into your inner being and offers up his toothy grin. We trust what he sees pleases him.

'It is man's
sympathy with
all creatures that
first makes him
truly a man.'
– *Dr Albert Schweitzer*

# Boots
## Start Thinking

His mother was a teddy bear and his father was a Mexican jumping bean. Don't believe us? Well, you have never met Boots! This feisty little fellow whose cuteness can be seen from the moon is guaranteed to bring a smile to the steeliest face. Found walking by the side of the road near Mildura in country Victoria, the tiny little Boer cross kid goat decided messing with cars was not a good idea. Assisted by the good folk from Victorian Dog Rescue, Boots literally hitchhiked his way to Edgar's Mission.

Determined to start changing people's attitudes towards farmed animals, Boots does not need a set of matches to spark that flame of compassion that lurks within us all. Just one meeting ought to do the trick. After all, the truth is that animals are emotional, intelligent, feeling beings regardless of the label we put on them. And just like Boots they all need our compassion, kindness and someone to walk all over.

Are you ready for Boots?

# Georgia
## Life with Brian

Horses have long been revered for their embodiment of strength, freedom and nobility. Yet despite the place horses hold in the hearts of many Australians they are valued more for what they can achieve for people rather than their intrinsic worth.

Georgia's story is typical of many of these noble beasts. With a distinct thoroughbred look, Georgia would have started out life rather well. Her owners probably had high hopes that she would be a racetrack sensation, bringing them glitz, glamour and financial rewards. However, like many a racehorse, Georgia could not live up to such lofty expectations and without an alternative career path, she found herself awaiting her turn in the knackery yard. Despite humans failing her, she placed her trust in the man who bought her a get-out-of-jail card; she endeared herself to the rescuers who just happened to be at the knackery yard at the right time. What better place to spend her twilight years than at Edgar's Mission.

When we arrived at the yard to pick up Georgia, we noticed a big robust bay gelding (castrated male horse) beside her; the two moved about the yard as one. Removing Georgia from the yard was problematic. We had to shut the gate on the gelding, pushing him back to stop him following his companion, his whinnies ringing in our ears as we loaded the obliging but anxious Georgia on to the horse trailer. We could see the frantic bay fellow racing up and down the fence line calling for his friend. How often do humans break up bonds between animals simply for convenience, yet herd animals like the horse form strong bonds that can last a lifetime.

Looking around the knackery yard it was hard not to despair at how we humans have betrayed these majestic animals. Pens of miniature ponies all squashed in together, faithful old and pitifully thin horses with neglect knots in their once beautiful flowing manes, bold standardbreds looking into distant paddocks they would never roam, terrified brumbies racing here and there, once proud thoroughbreds a shadow of their former selves and various other breeds simply surplus to the owners' needs. A pile of skeletons outside the kill floor served as a legacy to the morning's activities and will remain ingrained in our memories forever. Piles of heads in one section, legs and hooves in another: highly intelligent animals reduced to body bits like the assembly line of the automobile industry.

Seeing the bay gelding's head amongst this sorrowful site haunted our dreams that night and told us what we had to do the next day.

Our eyes filled with tears as we unloaded Brian the following day. Gentle Brian became a man on a mission as he carried his head high, and trotted proudly to his beloved Georgia. And as their nostrils touched, each letting out a gentle whinny, we knew we had done the right thing.

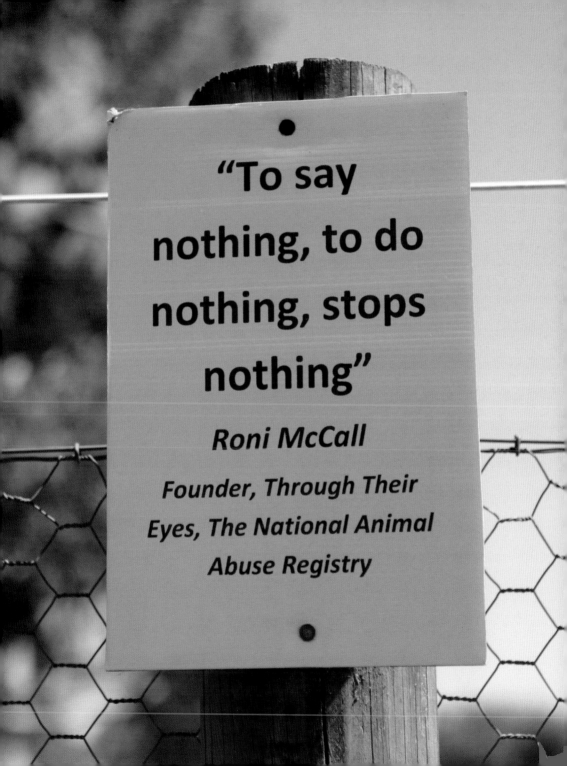

# Black Beauty

Back in 1877 a young devout Quaker girl named Anna Sewell was under the magical spell of equines as she penned what was to be one of the first animal rights novels, Black Beauty. At fourteen she sprained her ankle; it healed badly and coupled with a bone disease, Anna could never walk properly. She relied heavily on horse and cart as a means of transport. This brought her face-to-face with horses, and she saw the often careless and cruel treatment they received from humans. Anna was particularly appalled by the use of the bearing rein on carriage horses to make them keep their heads up and look pretty. Some horses were forced to work for hours in these devices, including having to try to pull loads uphill.

Anna only wrote one book; she died at 58, just months after its publication and never knowing the huge impact it would have on encouraging kindness, sympathy and understanding towards the treatment of horses and all animals. She would be proud to know that her central theme of a protest against many of the accepted but wrong practices of the time lead to the abolition of the cruel bearing rein, and that kicked off the animal rights movement. At Anna's funeral, her mother insisted that the uncomfortable bearing reins be removed from all the horses in the funeral procession.

Unfortunately today there still are dubious devices used on horses to alter their appearance or action. Many practices that cause unnecessary distress, discomfort or pain for animals are the result of ignorance or extreme lack of concern rather than deliberate acts of cruelty.

# 752 Lucky Hens
## A New Year's Resolution

'Can you please save my hens? I don't want them to go to slaughter.'

We never thought we'd hear these words from a one-time battery hen farmer but that is just what happened mid-2012. It resulted in Australia's largest rescue of farmed animals. Then in the dying days of 2012, we swung into action again when another farmer called to say he'd had enough. It was going to take some effort to pull this one off. With the festive season claiming many would-be helpers and battling against the rising temperatures that would make transporting the fragile hens prohibitive, we somehow made it happen.

The shed of despair was a heart-wrenching sight accompanied by the smell of pitiful creatures eking out an existence in tiny wire prisons amid the dust and 18 months' worth of excrement. Heads bobbed up and down, squawks rang out and curious gazes descended upon us.

The task was to remove the hens from the cages and pass them to others who would then ferry the liberated hens to the awaiting straw-lined

'Do something today which the world may talk about hereafter.'
– Admiral Collingswood

carriers and vehicles. Some hens required placement in our many hospital cages due to thinness, respiratory problems, eye infections or uterus conditions.

One by one, innocent creatures were granted a new lease on life. You would think the hens would appreciate getting out of such a hellhole but from their point of view, humans were bad news. For the past 18 months – the 'productive' lifespan of a battery hen – a human walking into the sheds was someone barely taking any notice of the chickens, every now and then removing a dead hen from a cage here, disposing of a near-dead one there and no doubt tossing about a few curses.

On this fateful day, hands gently reached inside the cages while kind voices cooed, 'Come here beautiful, I will save you.' Many of the hens attempted to flee while others froze in fear – it was heartbreaking. Moments later, the hen would blink in the sunshine for the first time in her life as she found her 'sea legs', tilting back and forth on solid ground, a welcome change from the sloping wire floor she had known. Overall these hens appeared in much better health than our first rescue, but they were riddled with lice. Each hen would need to be treated immediately on arrival at the sanctuary, prior to exiting the vehicle, essential to ensure our biosecurity would be maintained.

As the last hen was gently lifted from her cage we gave an exhausted but happy leap knowing that the tide was slowly turning. But in a glass-half-empty moment, we realised that while 752 hens got lucky, 752 baby roosters deemed unproductive were killed before they were 24 hours old. They remain the forgotten victims in this war.

Fast-forward to the glorious hens in their new home at Edgar's Mission. Some busily scratch about in the straw as others catch moments of sheer bliss when their dishevelled feathers feel the sun's unfamiliar rays. A little hen fastidiously grabs pieces of straw and tosses them onto her back while others have made fast work of finding a secret nest. The girls learned quickly that grains are delicious, as is our special mushy

mash. A sea of feathers and straw, not a cage in sight — you can almost breathe the hens' euphoria.

The wonderful thing about life is that there is always a time where we can say, 'I am not going to be a part of this anymore.' The hen farmer declared it on the eve of a New Year, and we would all do well to echo his words.

# The Lowdown on Chickens

Chickens are sociable animals who ideally live in stable groups, establishing an intricate social hierarchy known as a 'pecking order'.

Not only can chickens recognise the individual faces of up to 100 other birds in their flock, they can also recall where each of those individuals sit in the pecking order, relative to themselves.

Chickens are intelligent creatures with the cognitive ability to solve problems, recognise shapes and colours and can comprehend that objects still exist even after they are hidden from view. In this respect, they are more cognitively advanced than some small human children!

In 2002, the PBS documentary The Natural History of Chickens stated that, 'Chickens love to watch television and have vision similar to humans. They also seem to enjoy all forms of music, especially classical.'

Dust bathing is an activity that chickens will carry out daily in order to remain clean and well. The hens will crouch down in soil or litter and use their wings to distribute the matter over their body, which cleans feathers, prevents and removes parasites, removes oil build up and helps to maintain body temperature.

Hens are driven to lay their eggs in private, in a quiet and secluded place. If prevented from doing so, this frustrates a hen greatly.

Scratching in the soil, bathing in the sun, stretching their wings and preening feathers are all behaviours that make a chicken's life complete.

In Australia today, over 11 million egg-laying hens are confined within 'battery' cages, which allow them less space than the size of an A4 sheet of paper.

Since 2008, caged hens must be given at least 550 square centimetres of personal space. However researchers have found that to stretch her wings, a hen requires an average of 829 square centimetres and to preen, an average of 1150 square centimetres. The recommended cage size does not allow a hen to carry out her natural behaviour.

With no exercise, a battery hen can develop weak and brittle bones and is at a high risk of osteoporosis. More than 56 per cent of caged hens live with painful untreated fractures.

# Molly Brown
## The Unsinkable Sheep

Thursday 31 May 2012 was a night to remember for all the wrong reasons. A horrific truck rollover saw around 400 sheep fall onto the busy freeway below, leaving many dead and injured. People all around the globe reeled in horror at the images of the stricken sheep.

Molly Brown, so named after Titanic survivor, the unsinkable Margaret 'Molly' Brown, is thought to be the sole surviving sheep from the carnage. The truck had been abattoir bound, so Molly's uplifting story of beating the odds, not once but twice, hit the headlines as she recovered under the care of the Lost Dogs' Home in North Melbourne.

With her story reaching the masses and touching hearts, many dreamed that Molly would be rewarded for her bravery and her will to survive by living out the remainder of her days in a sheep's paradise. If Molly could speak 'human' she would no doubt have agreed; she had run for her life and fought against the odds because she believed that a better world for sheep was possible. And so, at Edgar's Mission, the dreams of one sheep and many people came true.

Molly's trip to the farm was like no other she had ever experienced. No multi-tiered, open-air livestock transporter for her but rather a custom fitted, temperature-controlled Kindness Van, complete with her very own ovine chaperone — the amazing ambassador sheep, Timmy. Molly Brown, the gentle Merino ewe, lives out her days surrounded by equally lucky sheep that have found solace at the sanctuary.

In April 2012, for every minute of every day, 47 sheep or lambs were slaughtered in Australia. These sheep were only ever known by a number and had never been considered anything other than a production unit. That one sheep managed to escape her predetermined fate has got to be a reason to never stop dreaming. Molly beating the odds on that fateful night gave people something to believe in, and served as a reminder that things can get better and that we can do better. People empathised with 'those poor sheep' and imagined what it would be like to be in a similar situation themselves. Those same people then came to understand what it means to be a sheep, a creature who feels fear, terror and panic just like us. Sheep want to see the sun shine, hang out with their buddies, eat when they are hungry, drink when thirsty and above all else, to feel safe.

Anyone who has had the opportunity to really get to know sheep understands they are intelligent, friendly and emotional animals. They can recognise the faces of their buddies, even after years, and can distinguish between friendly and gruff human expressions. They can learn their name and respond to it when called. Recent studies have shown that sheep have performed at a similar level to monkeys and humans in learning tasks, something many have never thought possible.

Molly has proved that the impossible is possible, given a chance.

DREAM AS
IF YOU'LL
LIVE
FOREVER,
LIVE AS IF
YOU'LL DIE
TODAY

JAMES DEAN

'Ideas are funny things.
They won't work unless you do.'

# Eliza & Emma

## Leaders of the Pack

Eliza and Emma escaped (with some friends) and rampaged through neighbouring gardens creating mess and mayhem as only pigs can do. They managed to capture media attention and were finally captured by the local animal control officers. As the story unfolded, they were claimed by the farmer who faced several thousands of dollars in restitution for the damage done by the marauding piggies.

Perhaps it was some kind of revenge by the recalcitrant pigs for the manner in which they had been used and the fate the farmer had intended for them. George Orwell chose well when he selected pigs to be the leaders of the farm. Sick of being continually impregnated and seeing their babies sold off, these mother pigs could endure no more, so trotting to the streets they oinked, 'We're mad as hell and we ain't going to take this anymore!'

The farmer surrendered these plucky porciner to our dear friends at Brightside Farm Sanctuary in Tasmania, then

Edgar's Mission came to the rescue. After a most eventful trans Bass Strait crossing, the two soon-to-be-mums found home sweet home, and settled in like they had lived there all their lives.

Pigs are really smart. They can play computer games and even out perform some chimpanzees in doing so. They quickly learn tasks like coming when called (although sometimes they choose to ignore this), sitting on command (although they don't like sitting on cold or uncomfortable surfaces) and hand, or rather trotter, shaking (but be warned, they are rather choosey who they greet like this). They can even work out how to open gates and where the feed room is. In other tests they have been taught the meaning of words and phrases and have been able to follow those instructions several years later. Oh, and the mums love to sing to their babies, just like humans do.

"Many have
forgotten this
truth, but you
must not forget it.
You remain
responsible,
forever, for what
you have tamed."

Antoine de Saint-Exupery
The Little Prince

# Hip-Hop Bob
## Professor Pig

Hip-Hop Bob's mother gave birth to her in a huge pile of perfectly placed straw. Her mum, Eliza, had spent many a painstaking hour getting it just right, moving a piece here, taking a mouthful there. Mother pigs naturally spend hours, even days, making a nest out of grass, branches, sticks and twigs to give their piglets somewhere safe to live when they are first born. Hip-Hop Bob popped out, blinking in the sunshine, breathing fresh air, sniffing all around, then immediately started looking for food. Pigs loooooooooooove food, and the piglet knew to crawl through the straw nest, over her mum's legs and around her seven siblings until she found one of her mum's teats. Each piglet claimed a teat, returning to it each feeding time.

Two days later, her mum's best friend Emma started making her nest, and Hip-Hop knew that her siblings would not be the only piglets in town anymore. They totalled sixteen.

As the piglets started to grow, so did their curiosity. They went on adventures around the farm, venturing a little further each day to see what was around the corner, but any sight or sound of human friends would send them scurrying back to the sanctity of their mothers. They'd put on their very best it-wasn't-me look.

One day they discovered a very convenient 'cat' door into the feed room. They snuck in, checking left and right to make sure no one spotted them. Bag upon bag of yummy delicious food were piled one

upon another reaching skyward. But how to get these sealed bags open? Well, the piglets had strength in numbers, eight on one side, eight on the other and one, two, three . . . pull! There was a rip . . . then again, one, two, three and there it was: 40 kilos of delicious oats poured out of the bag. Eureka! They rolled in it, slid in it, played in it, but then heard the screeching of metal as the feed room door slowly inched open. The piglets were dismayed that the humans proved smarter than they thought!

Not only are pigs really smart, they're really really fast and one by one they ran through the human legs, round the corner, under the fence and back to the safety of their pig house. Piglets 1; humans 0.

The piglets became famous and people came from everywhere to see them. On tours of the farm, they were used to teach people all about pigs. Each pig has a different personality, and is really not that different to a cats or a dog; they love to play and to hang out with friends and don't like being hurt. Pigs love mud, not because they are dirty animals, but because they cannot sweat; rolling about in the mud gives them a wonderful mud pack which in turn acts as a natural sunscreen and insect repellent. And pigs are the cleanest of animals, carefully choosing a toilet area and never going to the toilet close to where they sleep. They love to have their bellies rubbed, and did we mention that they're very smart? In fact they're smarter than many dogs. Studies have shown they can even outperform chimpanzees at computer games and Donald Broome, Professor of Animal Welfare, reckons they are as smart as a three-year-old child.

The pigs learned to sit — the people on the tours loved this. Hip-Hop and her buddies caught on pretty quickly; all they had to do was sit and they would be fed wheat biscuit after wheat biscuit after wheat biscuit. Piglets 2; Humans 0.

Hip-Hop Bob took a real shine to showing people how clever pigs are so she became an ambassador pig, travelling around Victoria as part of Edgar's Mission Kindness Tour. When she's not touring she hangs out with her buddies, Popcorn, Mikey, Polly and Rumpelstiltskin.

By the way, her full name is Hip-Hop Bob'stein. Like Einstein. Because she's so smart.

# The Lowdown on Sows

In Australia a Code of Practice allows pregnant pigs (sows) to be kept in tiny metal individual stalls measuring 2 metre long by 60 centimetres wide. This code protects industry operators from being prosecuted for cruelty. Tragically some 300,000 female breeding sows are kept inside sheds continually pregnant and severely confined, forced to stand or lie on hard floors. They can barely take a step forward or back. These animals produce the piglets destined to become bacon, ham and pork products.

Sows are extremely maternal. They will spend many hours making a nest for their piglets. In factory farming, mother pigs' natural instincts are frustrated. Just prior to giving birth they are moved to 'farrowing crates', a smaller area where their body is encircled by metal bars to even further limit their movement. With no straw for bedding, they give birth to their piglets on a hard floor. Nurturing and interacting with her young is impossible as the cruel metal frame imprisons her. Her young are removed after 3 or 4 weeks, she is impregnated again, and the cycle of suffering and deprivation continues.

As a result these gentle and intelligent creatures develop physical and psychological problems that wear them out before their time. They are 'rewarded' for their efforts by being sent to slaughter. Female pigs in factory farms are treated as breeding machines, enduring a cycle of suffering and deprivation. These 'sow stalls' have been banned in Britain for welfare reasons and are being phased out in the European Union.

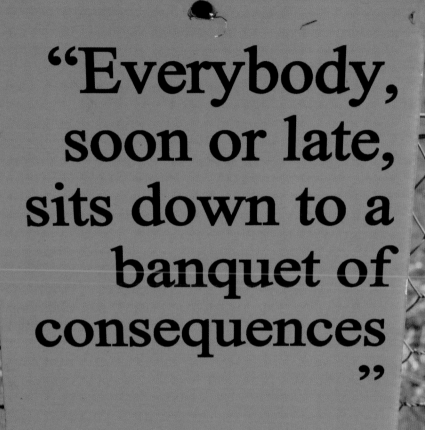

# Miss Marple
## Watching the Detective

It is a mystery that could well have been penned by the queen of crime writing, Agatha Christie. Just how could anyone allow a cow to fall into the dire condition of dear Miss Marple?

Day after painstaking day, the state of health of the sweet Hereford cross cow was deteriorating to the point where her skeletal form could barely muster the strength to walk, let alone eat. Miss Marple had dutifully served her human owners producing calf after calf, only to have them taken from her and fattened for slaughter, and had finally succumbed to the perils of old age and a tough life. Her last calf payed the ultimate price for its mother's ill health and lack of milk; it had died just days before we heard of Miss Marple's plight.

The farmer assured us that the cow identified with a number 5 ear tag in one ear and a floppy blue one in the other was just 'a little down in condition' and was 'six or seven years old'. We raised our eyebrows. At her new home, our suspicions were confirmed as we watched Miss Marple hoe into a biscuit of delicious green hay — our delight was tempered by the sight of mushed up green balls of saliva-encrusted grass being slowly spat out. A quick dental inspection revealed pale pink gums, the former home of long departed teeth. Determining the age of a cow by her teeth is not an exact science, but it's generally an effective method. Textbooks indicate that a 12-year-old cow would have worn down triangular-shaped teeth, and the smooth mouth of Miss Marple showed her to be closer to an incredible twenty years of age.

Miss Marple was suffering many physical woes and her eyes said she had just about given up but we picked up our magnifying glasses and began our detective work to give her the best possible chance of survival. Medication was administered to address her systemic infection and potions were mixed to arrest her debilitating diarrhoea. The race was on.

Miss Marple's appetite for oaten and lucerne chaff raised our hopes. Only days into her rehabilitation, she was flourishing, making fresh acquaintances during her daily wanders around the farm. This endearing old lady greeted each new pal demurely, in keeping with her namesake's character. The black chapter of her life closed forever.

Miss Marple proved to be sharp and clever, quickly learning where the cows hang out and how to give the most convincing pleading looks to receive bucketfuls of her favourite chaffy mix. She was friendly, gentle and, above all else, forgiving. We attributed that to her sweet soul, held prisoner to a tormented life. She never gave up hope that one day things would get better.

In saving Miss Marple we are doing far more than saving one cow; we are healing our own souls that ache with the knowledge that

innocent creatures like her have been condemned to a life where only profits and taste matter. Many people see cows in paddocks but on a whole they remain strangers to most of us — distant creatures in a bucolic landscape. Yet Miss Marple is possessed with her own unique and loveable personality, showing a willingness to explore, a desire to befriend and an appetite for love. Her undying resolve to hang in there despite formidable odds touches our hearts.

This grand old cow's story speaks to the goodness within us all who yearn for a non-violent world. It really shouldn't take a detective to make the connection between what is on our plates and what it means to creatures like Miss Marple for it to get there.

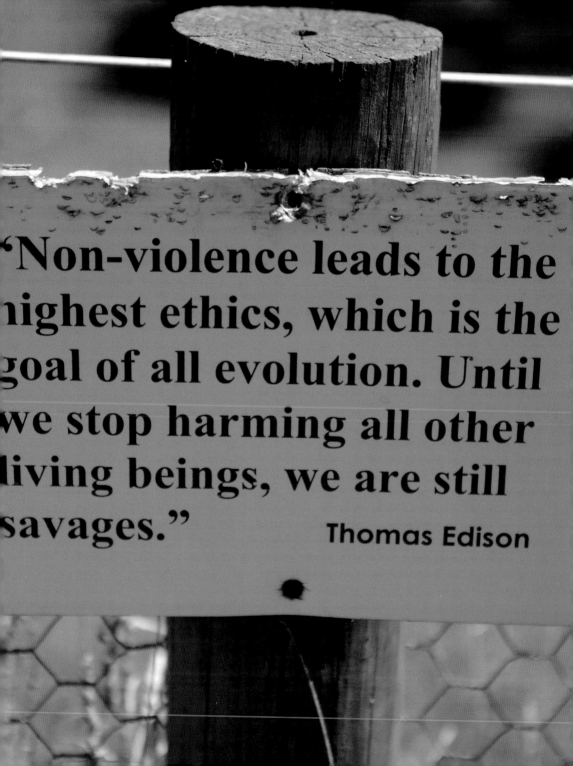

"Non-violence leads to the highest ethics, which is the goal of all evolution. Until we stop harming all other living beings, we are still savages."

Thomas Edison

# Timmy
## The Ambassador for Sheep

Timmy came to Edgar's Mission when he was only about one week old, a few days after some kind folk found him by the side of the road, tired and lonely. No one knows how he got there but perhaps he fell off the back of a truck. Timmy's natural charm and friendly nature quickly came to the fore and he become an ambassador for sheep, a voice for the millions of other lambs and sheep who were not as lucky as him. He's made many friends at markets and public events.

A recent scientific study lead by Keith Kendrick and a team of scientists from the Babraham Institute in Cambridge, England, revealed that sheep have specialised areas in the brain for facial recognition just like humans. They are capable of remembering the faces of up to 50 sheep for nearly two years. Sheep have been shown to prefer smiling human faces to stressed ones, with a preference for being around animals who are happy and contented. It would appear Charles Darwin got it right when he said the difference between us and animals was in degree, not kind.

# Brenda & Jacqui
## Rabbits with Wings

Brenda and her sister Jacqui are young and vibrant New Zealand White rabbits. They were born into this world as meat rabbits, kept within an intensive farming facility in Southern Tasmania. Destined for slaughter at just 10–12 weeks of age, kindness was a concept that looked certain to pass this adorable twosome by.

Their world was confined within a tiny wire cage suspended over a concrete floor, far removed from a rabbit's natural environment. So unnatural is it for a rabbit to remain standing on a harsh wire surface that Brenda's feet bore the evidence of the unimaginable pain this caused her. Too uncomfortable to stand or to sleep, Brenda lived each day on edge, unable to find any relief within her environment. Many of Brenda's companions showed physical signs of their discomfort. Untreated abscesses and infections were commonplace; eye and respiratory problems were also widespread within the rabbit 'factory' due to the build-up of faeces and the resulting ammonia.

Brenda's severe confinement not only lowered her immunity and compromised her physical wellbeing but it also lead to psychological stress. The denial of her most basic instincts such as burrowing, mutual grooming and exploring her world led Brenda to become bored and frustrated within her tiny prison.

Fortunately the rabbit farm was closed down and, for the first time in her life, Brenda, experienced the power of kindness. Big Ears Farm Sanctuary came to the rescue. Then proving rabbits can indeed have wings, Brenda and Jacqui were flown to Victoria to begin a life of luxury at Edgar's Mission.

With not a cage in sight, Brenda now proudly explores her new forever home – a bunny's paradise. Instead of cold and harsh wire, the warm, soft earth now caresses her feet, which scratch and dig until her heart is content. Her diet is no longer the result of a carefully calculated feed-to-weight conversion ratio but is made up of a variety of the freshest fruits and vegetables, all carefully selected and distributed so that each meal becomes a treasure-hunting taste sensation. Friends are now close by for mutual grooming and companionship, basking in the sun. Brenda and her buddies have established an intricate warren system beneath their home, freely following instincts once so frustrated by their confinement.

Life for Brenda and Jacqui is now far better than they ever dreamed possible. Facilities such as the factory farming system where they resided were prohibited throughout Australia until 1987 and are still outlawed in both the Northern Territory and Queensland. Unfortunately for Brenda and her bunny brethren, the intensive farming of rabbits for meat is an industry that is largely unheard of within the general public. This means the truth about the industry is hidden and there is rarely a light at the end of these rabbits' incredibly dark and bleak tunnel of life.

On 80–100 rabbit farms in Australia there are over 120,000 bunnies who will never be touched by kindness in the way Brenda has been. Or will they? The choice is yours.

'Never doubt that a small group of thoughtful, committed citizens can change the world; indeed, it is the only thing that ever does.'

*Margaret Mead*

# Ruby
## The Right Job for a Dog

Ruby is a purebred working sheep dog. Her previous owner paid a lot of money for her as a pup, so his expectations were very high. Some people believe that you can put a value on animals but Ruby couldn't understand what exactly was wanted of her. Her lack of ability made her owner very cross. He said she was a bad dog and he beat her, trying to get her to understand. This confused the poor dog even more.

Deep down Ruby always wanted to have fun; she never wanted to herd sheep and spoil their fun either. They looked like they enjoyed hanging out together and the last thing they wanted was a dog hassling them. But her owner didn't see it like that. He would rant and rave at her until one day he said he had had enough and took Ruby to his mate's place to shoot her. She got very scared and wet herself; she did that a lot whenever people raised their voices or their hands — she would cower in fright, fearing the worst.

She knew the man with the gun had a good heart deep down,

and sensed just that some hearts sleep more than others. She thought if she could awaken his sleeping heart he might just spare hers. When he got his gun, she jumped up on him. She knew she wasn't meant to but she wanted to take one last look into his eyes and maybe, just maybe she could see into his heart. A tear filled his eye as he said, 'Down dog, down.' He walked away and made a phone call.

The rest is the start of Ruby's life at Edgar's Mission. The gate was opened to her, along with our hearts. To repay this kindness, she made it her official duty to personally greet every visitor, both human and non-human, to Edgar's Mission, ensuring that there was never any doubt that they would feel the gentle touch (or in her case, lick) of kindness. And who knows, she might even wake up a few more hearts along the way.

# Snuffles

## The Gift Pig

At just 3.5 months old, Snuffles tipped the scales at 13 kilos, but only time would tell if she truly remained miniature in size. Snuffles was purchased as a gift for a couple who were not ready to be pig parents and they quickly surrendered the adorable young porcine to a shelter.

Still unsure of the world — after all, hers had just been turned upside down — Snuffles was a little aloof at first but quickly melted in our arms. She enjoyed a cuddle and good old snuffle. Her favourite treats were watermelon (which doubled as a neat wallow) and grapes. Snuffles quickly mastered the sit-and-be-cute command, affirming what fast learners pigs are. Pigs are so much more than a token gift.

While Snuffles' journey from unwanted present to adored friend had a happy ending, not all animals given as gifts will be so lucky. Her story serves as a timely reminder to never surprise someone with an animal. But one thing is for sure: Snuffles is the gift that keeps on giving as she made her way into many hearts.

# Alexander the Great

## A Tribute to Kindness

You could be forgiven for thinking it is the enormous size of Alexander the rooster that makes him great. He is certainly a huge bird, tipping the scales at over 9 kilos, but it is his wonderful naturally cheerful personality that seals his greatness.

Alexander is a broiler chicken. As with all farm animals, their existence is to fulfil a purpose. In the case of a broiler chicken, that purpose is to be killed so their flesh can be used for meat production. But Alexander got lucky. On the fateful day that would have been his last, a Good Samaritan took pity on the confused and bewildered bird on the side of the road.

While Alexander will never quite know what divine intervention it was, he is thankful to have the opportunity to see out the remainder of his days at Edgar's Mission. He has made new friends with other equally

lucky broiler chickens, turkeys, ex-battery hens and factory-farmed rabbits. He is now on a special diet, created not with cold calculations but with the utmost love, to help with his burgeoning weight. Mealtimes are filled with delicious healthy treats such as watermelon, lettuce, grapes, bok choy and corn on the cob. Alexander loves the feeling of scratching around in the soil and bathing in the dust. He loves the warm rays of the sun as he lies on his side. He loves the caress of his soft, clean straw bed. He loves the sensation he gets when his big feet wrap around the wooden perch that his human friends have made especially low for him.

We have come to know and love Alexander the Great, he of great tragedy, he of great triumph and with a story of great kindness. We see him as so much more than the 'before' of a chicken nugget.

# The Lowdown on Broiler Chickens

A broiler chicken is another name for a chicken raised for meat. From go to a very short whoa, the life of a broiler chicken is anything but natural. Hatched from an incubator, rapidly growing broiler chickens reach their slaughter weight of just under 2 kilos in five to seven weeks, three times their natural growth rate. In 2010–11, 491 million broiler chickens did just this. Selectively bred for rapid growth, huge muscle mass and quick feed conversion, these intelligent, sensitive and inquisitive birds pay an enormous price for human ingenuity. Their Frankenstein world is purely of human design.

Vast windowless sheds commonly house around 40,000 birds, whose unnatural growth rate places enormous pressure on their hearts, lungs and immature immune systems. Many die of starvation because they grow too slowly to reach the raised feed or water stations, or because they are unable to stand due to lameness. Lameness is a huge welfare issue plaguing broiler chickens with bone fractures and dislocations not uncommon, as are hock burns that occur because the broilers are forced to live in the accumulation of ammonia-rich chicken excrement. Air quality is diminished for this same reason, resulting in respiratory and eye problems. It should come as no surprise that 20 million chickens never even make it to their target weight.

With no natural sunlight, soil or fresh air, there is little kindness in the life of a broiler chicken. Once the chickens reach their target weight they are collected by chicken catchers in what is generally a rough and hurried process. Five chickens will be ferried in each hand to tiny cages where the terrified birds will be crammed before they are trucked off to an abattoir for slaughter. For these pitiful birds, it will be the only time in their life they will see daylight and smell clean air. The slaughtering process is anything but pleasant as birds are shackled upside down by their legs onto an overhead conveyor belt that will take them to the killing room.

# Humphrey & Doris
## Coming Home

Behind Humphrey's sad old eyes lies a gentle goat, perhaps even a friendly goat if given half the chance. Yet with shaggy overgrown angora fleece and hooves so long they curled back like elves' slippers, he told a tale of a life forgotten. His buddy Doris, a much younger female goat, showed no inkling of trust and her deft turn of speed when in retreat said none was to be forthcoming soon.

Both Humphrey and Doris, along with their sheepy friend Loppy, were once 'owned' by a lady whose heart was bigger than her means. The trio had moved from rental property to rental property, with no place to call home. With a future that looked bleak, their eventual surrender to Edgar's Mission meant that a life on the move was finally to become a thing of the past.

With Humphrey's fleece shorn, his pitiful condition brought tears to our eyes; his lice-ridden emaciated body made us fear we were too late to save him. In conditions such as his, organ shut down is never too far away. Lice treatment administered, drenching complete, a lovely warm jacket donned and a delicious and nutritious diet commenced, it was now up to Humphrey.

While Humphrey was ribby and thin, Doris was portly and rotund, beyond what a grass-fed goat should be. A veterinary examination revealed that Doris had been keeping company with more than just Humphrey. We raced against time to prove ourselves worthy of Doris's trust before we heard the pitter patter of tiny kid hooves and their demanding bleats for attention.

We continue to provide sanctuary for Humphrey, for Doris and for her babies, and they will know only love, happiness and kindness for the rest of their days.

'How wonderful it is that nobody need wait a single moment before starting to improve the world.'

– *Anne Frank*

# Xena and Daffy

## Lucky Ducks

Xena and Daffy were most fortunate to have escaped the grisly fates that awaited them.

Friendly Xena, flying over neighbourhood fences and taunting dogs, was rescued by a caring soul who took her to a local vet clinic. Dear little Daffy was purchased from a livestock market and taken to be raised as a child's pet in suburbia.

Thankfully for Daffy, her human carers quickly realised that a life spent caged within a suburban backyard is no life at all for a duck and decided to surrender her to a local animal rescue charity. Alas, the organisation was all too familiar with such stories and was already overrun with unwanted and unclaimed cats and dogs. The best they could offer was three days in a holding pen. Unless a new home was found in that time, life would be no more for Daffy. Horrified at the fate awaiting the young duck, frantic calls were made until the number of Edgar's Mission was found.

While we were very pleased to offer a safe, secure and happy life to Xena and Daffy, it is disturbing that all too often people dive in the deep end of pet ownership and do not fully consider the quality of life — or lack thereof — that they are able to afford gentle little souls like these two.

If only all animals could fly off safely into the wide blue yonder … But until that day comes along, their only hope for a life worth living remains with us. By just opening our eyes and listening to our hearts we may just hear the drumbeat of a kindred spirit begging for mercy. Or it might just be the dog scratching at the door for dinner. Either way, you're the one who can make a difference …

'All the darkness in the world cannot put out the light of a single candle.'

# Tammy
## The Medieval Sheep

Tammy arrived at the Edgar's Mission in the arms of a Good Samaritan who had found her. She was severely malnourished, dehydrated, flystruck and suffering from scabby mouth. Weighing less than 10 kilos on arrival, Tammy was too weak to stand; she was immediately placed on a drip and given antibiotics and we waited.

Tammy's road to recovery was particularly rough, and she suffered many setbacks along the way. A wonderful WWOOFer (willing worker on organic farm) staying with us at the time spent countless hours working with Tammy, massaging her joints, providing vital physiotherapy, picking grass and even chipping in with the nightly task of checking and moving Tammy about to ensure she did not get pressure sores or place undue stresses on her rumen (first part of her stomach).

Sheep are ruminants and they make a lot of gas in their stomachs from chewing grass. You can often hear a sheep burping and it's very important for them to do so. It is also equally important that sheep do not lie on their sides for lengthy periods or roll onto their backs as this can cause their stomachs to invert, causing a build up of gas. The consequences of this are very serious and can include heart failure and death.

They say that necessity is the mother of invention and this was so true in Tammy's case. One of her hind legs had atrophied and would buckle under her weight. We needed to devise a way to offer the joint support and provide her with a means of mobility until she could regain her strength. To this end, we fashioned what looked like some medieval contraption, but it certainly did the trick. Soon Tammy was able to stand unassisted and her curiosity grew each day. Wandering further and further, we had to keep a watchful eye on her lest she fall and be unable to regain her balance.

But Tammy's spirit was stronger than any of her ailments and her determination to live quickly transformed her from a frail little soul to a confident, happy girl demanding more wheat biscuits.

Anyone can give up, it's the easiest thing in the world to do. But to hold it together when everyone else would understand if you fell apart, that's true strength"

# Blossom

## One is the Loneliest Number

Dear little Blossom was all alone in a paddock, her big brown eyes bulging out from under the longest white eyelashes as she stretched her head and neck skyward. A moo, as feeble as it was innocent, escaped as she cried out for a mother who would never return. As the mercury climbed, so too did the concern of a Good Samaritan whose heart and ears heard the pleading calls of the tiny week-old calf. Determined to not bear witness to the painfully slow death of an innocent creature, a call was made to the farmer. 'You can have 'er, she's no use to me,' came the gruff reply. Bundling up the precious brown-and-white girl who still smelled of her mother's milk, Blossom was one step closer to a life worth living.

If the farmer's voice was steely and cold, the next voice Blossom would hear was gentle and welcoming. With her severely sunburnt nose and pleading eyes fixed upon us, the words, 'How you could anyone deprive this baby of its mother?' rolled from our lips as our hearts and actions raced to combat her dehydration.

Offering Blossom a special formula in what would have seemed a most unlikely looking udder, we apologised that we were not her mummy but assured her we would do our very best to care for her. We whispered that we would ensure she would never again be the loneliest number.

If nature has her way, the bond between a cow and her calf is very strong and continues after the calf is fully grown. Mother cows are fiercely protective of their young; some will even nurse their calves for up to a year. But sadly, few are given the chance. Dairy calves are separated shortly after birth so the mother's milk can be harvested for human consumption, while beef calves like Blossom are generally weaned at 8-10 months of age. But for Blossom, there will be no separation from her new friends as she finds fields to conquer and dreams to live out as her life blooms into all it should be.

'The worst sin towards our fellow creatures is not to hate them, but to be indifferent to them, that's the essence of inhumanity.'

– *Isaac Bashevis Singer*

# Melvin

## The Life Changer

Left for dead in a ditch by the side of the road amongst the dead bodies of his companions, little Melvin somehow found the will to survive. But he couldn't do it alone. By some divine intervention a council roadside worker came upon the grizzly scene along the little-used road and both lives would change for the better. Shaking his head in disbelief, he thought he saw something moving. Taking a second look, nothing moved, but just as his heavy heart told him to move on a tiny 'baa' pierced his soul and he saw the young wether. 'I couldn't leave the little blighter there, could I?' he would later say.

The lamb who would be named Melvin was a severely underweight and recently shorn Merino, with infected sores from where he lay. The only movement the poor little chap could muster was to lift his head. It took the love, kindness and ingenuity of the worker and his wife to get Melvin on the road to recovery. Quickly fashioning a sling to keep the resilient Melvin upright would prove lifesaving; sheep left on their sides for too long will succumb to bloat, a condition that results in breathing difficulties and often death.

Melvin rallied with physiotherapy, glucose-filled syringes, manual feeding of grass and hay along with all the love the Good Samaritans could muster. While it took some days for him to gain the strength to walk again, Melvin would soon befriend the family dogs. Seeing the lamb happily playing in the yard with their pets caused the line between friend and food to blur. The couple soon realised that their work was done and a new home was needed for Melvin. Their hearts sank when they considered that life on farms means an untimely end and a conversion into the Sunday roast if you are a sheep.

News of Melvin's recovery was shared with friends who mentioned Edgar's Mission Farm Sanctuary. At first they were incredulous at the thought of a farm that would provide sanctuary and a long and happy life, not only for sheep but all farmed animals. It seemed too good to be true. But that was before they made the trek to Edgar's Mission. The tear-filled eyes of the wife and beaming smile of the worker bear testament that Edgar's Mission changes more than the lives of the animals who are fortunate to find their way to us.

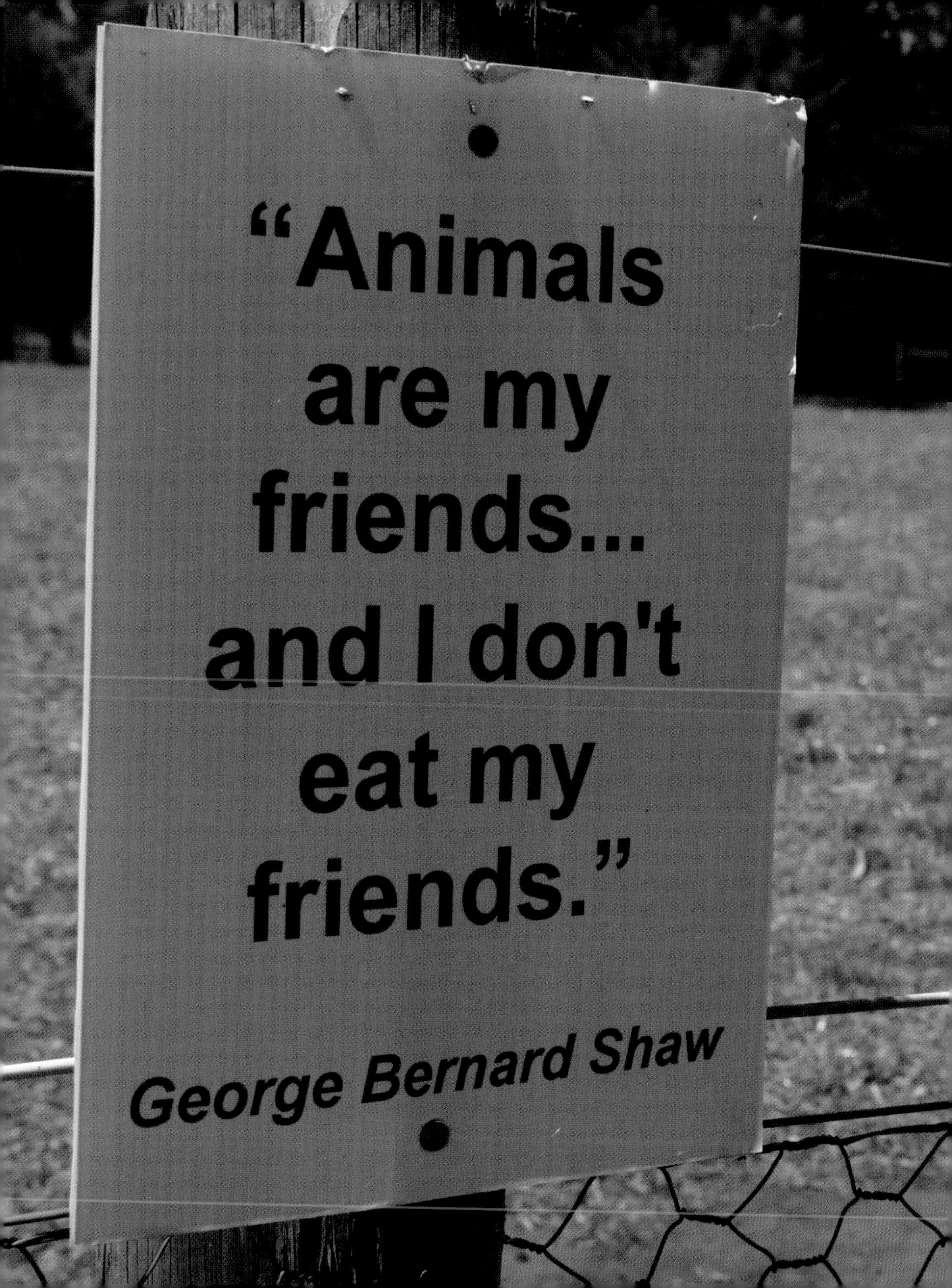
"Animals
are my
friends...
and I don't
eat my
friends."
George Bernard Shaw

# Jessie & Destiny
## Motherly Love

Jesse James, the infamous American outlaw, rode into town in the 1800s, robbing banks and trains and causing much mayhem. When little Jessie Pony trotted her way to Edgar's Mission, she stole our hearts.

In a world where equines can fetch prices of several millions of dollars, a horse's worth is largely determined by what it can contribute to the lives of those who claim 'ownership' of them. Miniature ponies like little Jessie can command a huge price tag, yet Jessie's owners considered her unworthy of their efforts to catch her when she escaped from her breeder into parklands. Standing just 8.3 hands tall (that's 89 centimetres in human terms) Jessie eluded capture for quite some time, earning her great notoriety.

Jessie's experience had taught her that humans were not to be trusted and it took the dart gun and a posse of good-hearted people headed by a veterinarian to rein Jessie in. The heavily sedated pony was carried to a float and transported to the local pound to be auctioned

off as unclaimed livestock. Things were looking grim for Jessie — no one wanted the wayward pony.

At Edgar's Mission, we believed Jessie was priceless. She was adorable and fought for her life just as we would if faced with such formidable foes. Over and over, situations like this remind us of the commonality we have with non-human animals: we all share the same need for food and water, safety and comfort and a place to call home. Jessie began to trust us.

One morning on our rounds, we were greeted by a tiny little bundle of black-and-white cuteness, confirming our suspicions that Jessie's ever-growing belly was more than just a legacy of the good feed she had been receiving.

Motherly love reigns supreme and Jessie dutifully protected her baby and confirmed what commonsense and science tell us: animals, just like humans, love, protect and seek only the best for their young. We sat, eyes agog, watching the proud mother ushering her baby around the paddock as the many curious non-human neighbours looked on, awaiting their introduction. And as we sat, we pondered; was it good luck or providence that guided Jessie to us? It was in this moment that the name of Jessie's girl came to us — Destiny.

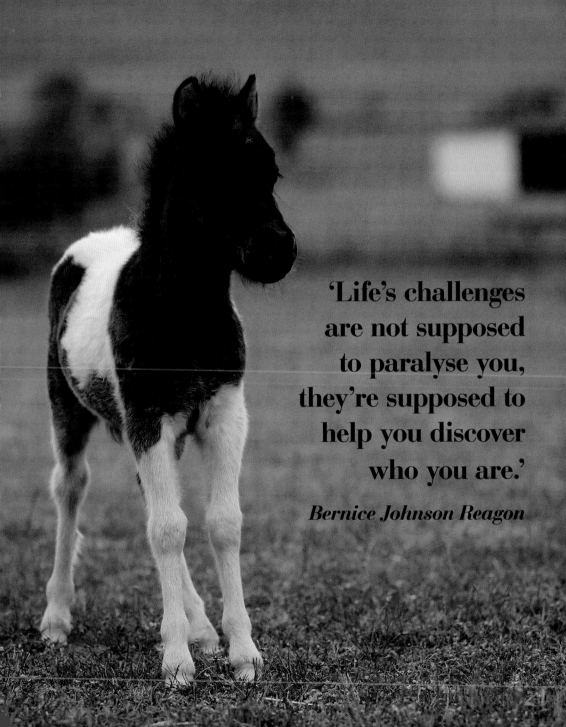

'Life's challenges
are not supposed
to paralyse you,
they're supposed to
help you discover
who you are.'

*Bernice Johnson Reagon*

# Bluey
## Hey True Blue

Bluey is a real Aussie battler. With his ruggedly handsome good looks, his striking crown of red and his battle-worn blind eye, he represents the true spirit of Australia — he has shown grit and determination to fight on, regardless of the odds. Despite his personable nature, Bluey was cast out on the streets, with no place to call home. He drew on all his survival skills just to stay alive. He is the truest of underdogs and he is a rooster.

Bluey's gender alone was enough to bring about his demise, but this rooster would have none of it, cheating death on several occasions. His number was just about up when he happened to peck on the door of a kindly elderly lady. Touched by his plucky resolve and feeling pity for the rooster with one blind eye, it was a teary and world-weary voice that begged us to give Bluey one more chance.

Roosters are dealt one of the greatest raw deals of all in our community, yet so few people are aware of their plight. Nature dictates that around 50 per cent of all chicks born will be male and therefore millions are killed before they live one day. Why? Roosters are simply of no use to the egg industry, where millions of chickens are hatched in the name of food production. And when a school hatching project morphs into a vocal testosterone-charged rooster, the humble rooster is shunned again by unappreciative neighbours and suburban councils.

Yet given the chance, roosters are as adorable as they are clever, as endearing as they are protective of their kind and as loyal as they are wise — qualities us humans could do well to emulate.

Hey True Blue — let's make kindness to all a big part of the hallmark of being Australian.

"A journey of
a thousand
miles begins
with a single
step"

*Lao Tzu*
*(China Taoist philosopher BC 600)*

# Acknowledgements

I trust that reading *The Gift of Kindness* has informed, inspired and empowered you to recognise that kindness is the basis upon which a better world can evolve for the future generations of all species. Most importantly, I hope I have shown you that it is possible for each and every one of us to contribute to that goal.

And it is due to the kindness of others that this book has come to life. My unending thanks go to each and every person who has made this possible. I thank Lyn White, who turns out not to be the simple 'office gal' I thought she was when my dear friend Glenys Oogjes (to whom I also owe a debt of gratitude) sent her along to assist my animal advocacy campaign at local government level several years ago. I recall how my heart sank as I sat down before chambers, waiting for the fresh new recruit of Animals Australia to champion the cause of circus animals (praying all the while she at least knew the issues). However, before Lyn's first sentence was complete, I knew I was not only in the presence of one of the greatest animal advocates of all time but that I was also in the company of someone who would soon become one of my dearest friends and greatest mentors.

I will be forever indebted to the kindness of Shirley Brine, a wonderful woman who has dedicated her life to improving the welfare of animals and who, without having ever met me, made a significant donation to help create Edgar's Mission, securing a brighter future for all of its residents. To Bunty Jackson, whose love of animals is well known and who came on board pretty much from day one to painstakingly keep our financial records balanced and up to date.

To Kyle, Paula, Meg, Tash, Peter and Kerri who currently make Team Edgar happen. For your patience, kindness and understanding, I thank you from the bottom of my heart. To my dear friend Robyn for believing in me and to Diana and Cherie who have always been on hand to heed my call for help, thank you all. Thanks also to Ben and Lindsay whose creativity and kindness have provided Edgar's Mission with an exciting and inviting new dimension. A special note of thanks goes to my dear friend Kyle; although we are worlds apart, we somehow make a magical team. Special thanks to the incredible Paula — a younger, prettier, smarter version of myself — who has learned to judge my tiredness by the number of typos I make in the many stories I forward to her for editing. I have great faith that the future of Edgar's Mission will be in good hands with Kyle and Paula at the helm.

To the wildly witty and adorable Marieke Hardy for guiding me to Penguin Books and who, ably assisted by Michaela McGuire, created *Women of Letters*, which has not only reignited the lost art of letter writing but has also contributed significant funds to Edgar's Mission. To Andrea McNamara and the team at Penguin, many thanks for your understanding, for your belief in my work and, of course, for accommodating an adorable goat in your office during a meeting.

To my mum, thanks for encouraging my love of animals and the natural world and for so willingly turning her bathroom into a nursery for lambs, kid goats and whatever other species that happened to require my care. My dad has sadly passed on and will never get to see the legacy of his final act of kindness to me.

My thanks indeed to our dedicated veterinary team of Tam and Dr Cat, who are always on hand to treat our farm animal friends as some *one* not some thing. It is difficult to put into words the depth of gratitude myself and all those in the animal protection movement owe to the inimitable Phil and Trix Wollen; their kindness knows no borders.

I will be forever profoundly grateful to the many volunteers and supporters, both past and present, whose belief in my work has ensured the physical and financial viability of Edgar's Mission. There truly can be no greater gift to bestow or to receive than kindness.

But most of all, I thank the animals who I have been fortunate to know and love and, in many instances, say goodbye to. You have enriched my life in ways I can never describe and you have shown me that regardless of the form we take in this world, we all need, seek and respond to kindness.

Visit **www.edgarsmission.org.au** to find out more about our work and how to support the animals.

# Sources

The information in this book comes from the following sources:

Meat and Livestock Australia: www.mla.com.au

Department of Environment and Primary Industries: www.dpi.vic.gov.au

Department of Agriculture, Fisheries and Forestry: www.daff.gov.au

Animals Australia: www.animalsaustralia.org

Australia Turkey Farming: Big Birds, Big Cruelty:
www.bigbirdsbigcruelty.org

# Credits

PENGUIN

Published by the Penguin Group
Penguin Group (Australia)
707 Collins Street, Melbourne, Victoria 3008, Australia
(a division of Pearson Australia Group Pty Ltd)
Penguin Group (USA) Inc.
375 Hudson Street, New York, New York 10014, USA
Penguin Group (Canada)
90 Eglinton Avenue East, Suite 700, Toronto, Canada ON M4P 2Y3
(a division of Pearson Penguin Canada Inc.)
Penguin Books Ltd
80 Strand, London WC2R 0RL England
Penguin Ireland
25 St Stephen's Green, Dublin 2, Ireland
(a division of Penguin Books Ltd)
Penguin Books India Pvt Ltd
11 Community Centre, Panchsheel Park, New Delhi – 110 017, India
Penguin Group (NZ)
67 Apollo Drive, Rosedale, Auckland 0632, New Zealand
(a division of Pearson New Zealand Ltd)
Penguin Books (South Africa) (Pty) Ltd
Rosebank Office Park, Block D, 181 Jan Smuts Avenue, Parktown North, Johannesburg, 2196, South Africa
Penguin (Beijing) Ltd
7F, Tower B, Jiaming Center, 27 East Third Ring Road North, Chaoyang District, Beijing 100020, China

Penguin Books Ltd, Registered Offices: 80 Strand, London WC2R 0RL, England

First published by Penguin Group (Australia), 2013

1 3 5 7 9 10 8 6 4 2

Text and photographs © Edgar's Mission 2013

The moral right of the author has been asserted

Cover photographs by Kyle Behrend
Cover design by Adam Laszczuk © Penguin Group Australia
Text design by Pauline Haas © Penguin Group Australia
Typeset in Mrs Eaves by Pauline Haas
Colour reproduction by Splitting Image Colour Studio Pty Ltd, Clayton, Victoria
Printed and bound in China by South China Printing Co Ltd

National Library of Australia Cataloguing-in-Publication data:
Ahern, Pam, author.
The gift of kindness / by Pam Ahern; photographs by Kyle Behrend.

9780143570905 (paperback)
Edgar's Mission.
Livestock—Victoria—Pictorial works.
Livestock—Victoria—Anecdotes.
Domestic animals—Victoria—Pictorial works.
Domestic animals—Victoria—Anecdotes.
Animal rescue—Victoria—Anecdotes.
Animal sanctuaries—Victoria—Pictorial works.
Behrend, Kyle, photographer.
636.0887

penguin.com.au